What the Experts Are Saying about
How to Jump-Start Your Career

"This is a perfect, uplifting, useful book for all times! Hemmings starts with a invaluable idea: "Everyone sells something. Everyone has to communicate." and then plays it out with a series of entertaining anecdotes and examples that enlighten, educate and inspire. Whether we're a leader or the led, a peon or a potentate, a seller or a buyer, a parent, teacher or student, this book will help you communicate with and influence others more effectively."

Dr. Tony Alessandra
Author of *The Platinum Rule, Communicating at Work* and *The NEW Art of Managing People*

"Robert Hemmings' book is a must read for any businessperson who is interested in improving their life. You are drawn in by the success stories of master sales professionals and think you are reading about improving one's abilities at selling and suddenly you realize you are learning to improve the whole of your life.

Who cannot benefit from improving their ability to master the art and the science if communication? This book should be required reading for all undergraduates in almost any field of study and especially for graduate students in MBA programs and those in law schools.

Mr. Hemmings should get a Ph.D. in the science of persuasion. His lifelong study is a significant scholarly achievement. He was forged in the crucible of the Great Depression and his timeless teachings are as relevant now as ever.

I could not put the book down. I have read every word more than once and will read it again. I hope my students read it and I pray my children and grandchildren study this important work.

Buy it for someone whose life you want to improve and they will thank you for it. Read it yourself and you may also become a Master Communicator as is Mr. Hemmings and are his many devoted students."

Duke K. Bristow, Ph.D.
Associate Professor of Clinical Finance and Economics
Marshall School of Business
University of Southern California

"Bob Hemmings has a down-to-earth way of helping you see the value of a positive attitude, strong speaking and listening skills and perseverance. And you don't have to be a salesman to benefit from this book. Well done."

Larry Earley
Family and Relationship Coach

"I thoroughly enjoyed this book. It has valuable information I can use in both my personal and professional life. As a Jr. High School teacher, I feel better equipped to communicate with my students and to be a more effective communicator and teacher. I think it would be a beneficial read for all teachers. The stories are entertaining and helped pull it all together—this made the book "Fun to Read.""

Ms. Mary Ashley
Roy, Utah

"What a potent combination—communication tips and selling secrets that can make you a winner! Put this book on the list of things you wish you learned in college. Words can work wonders to change your life, and this book shows you exactly how to do it."

Jim Kobs
Author, *Profitable Direct Marketing*

"Bob Hemmings makes owning his book worthwhile within the first two chapters: With studied casualness he points out that people buy from you for two reasons. He then names the reasons, and they're just two of the huge load of usable and practical nuggets he supplies, clearly and with his famous good nature making his message a delight. Lots, lots to benefit from in these pages. Thank you, Bob!"

Herschell Gordon Lewis
Author, *On the Art of Writing Copy*

"This book is a masterful job of showing the relationship between selling and a way of living an enjoyable and successful financial life. A 'must read' for those who are interested in both."

> Fred W. Mackenbach
> Retired President and COO,
> The Lincoln Electric Company, Cleveland, Ohio.

"I like books that tell stories. The more the better. Stories teach and Hemmings' remembrances and stories are worth as much to college grads as to those in the work-force who wonder why they aren't getting ahead. I like to underline and review the wisdom. In this case I have ten pages of quotes and notes. There are 12 action packed chapters, but Chapter Six, with the 12 Cardinal Rules from the master is the gold. I carry them with me every day."

> James W. Obermayer
> CEO, Sales Lead Management Association

"Throughout my many years in business (from bottom to top) it was suggested to me and confirmed many times that in business as in life the only real problems we face are 'people problems.' Bob Hemmings has addressed this fact many times in his book entitled Jump-Start Your Life. However, much more importantly, he offers anecdotes based on personal and researched experiences that would be a blessing to any reader of his text. Always remember, good communication is the key."

> Jon T. Pawley
> President (Ret.), a Portland Cement Company,
> subsidiary of CEMEX

"This book is chock-full of "Un" Common Sense and State-of-the-Art Wit and Wisdom from a true Master Communicator and Star Salesman. Bob Hemmings has distilled a lifetime (90 years + and counting!) of lessons learned into an inspirational guide to a successful life."

> Walter Rose
> Entrepreneur, Business Executive, Community Leader

"What a wise and witty book! Thanks to Bob Hemmings's decades of honing his natural gifts in persuasive communications, Jump-Start Your Career is a gem of a resource for business people—and not just those at the outset of their careers. I am grateful he took the time to get it all down on paper. And especially that he packed it with entertaining anecdotes about communications strategies we can emulate—and aspire to."

    Ruth P. Stevens
    President, eMarketing Strategy
    Adjunct Professor, Columbia Business School

To Suzi
a loosely lady
Bob Hemmings

HOW TO JUMP-START YOUR CAREER

Discover the Secrets of How to Become a Master Communicator

Robert L. Hemmings

RĀCOM
COMMUNICATIONS

Chicago, Illinois

Copyright © 2011 by Robert L. Hemmings

Editor: Richard Hagle
Cover and interior design by Sans Serif, Inc., Saline, MI

Published by:
Racom Books/Racom Communications
150 N.Michigan Ave.
Suite 2800
Chicago, IL 60601
312-494-0100 / 800-247-6553
www.racombooks.com

ISBN 978-1-933199-27-6

I dedicate this book to my good friend
and confidant Michael McCully.
Mike's confidence inspired me to write it
and his continual pushing and prodding
compelled me to finish it.

*A special thanks to my daughter Jill Coddington
for her proofreading and editing skills.*

Contents

Foreword

The professor walked across the classroom, lecture notes tucked under his arm. At the podium he shuffled his lecture notes and then leaned forward and offered a pleasant "Good morning."

The students responded, and the professor continued, saying, "As graduate students I know why you are here. You are taking this course in Entrepreneurship because you have graduated from college and want to use your new-learned skills to start you own business."

After seeing the students give a silent nod of agreement, he resumed, "Just to be sure we are all on the same wave length, I'd like to ask a few questions. Please respond by raising your hand." Then he asked, "How many of you want to make money and become wealthy?" Every hand shot up. In quick order, he posed three more questions:

1. How many want to be captains of industry?
2. How many would like to build a business that would sell at twenty times earnings?
3. How many want to build a business that can survive and thrive in good and bad times?

Every hand waved in total agreement.

But, to the final question there was a less than enthusiastic response. When asked, "How many of you want to be salespeople?" only a few hands were raised.

Before addressing the class, the professor slowly scanned the students, then responded by saying, "Sales is the catalyst that makes any business profitable."

He reinforced his statement with, "Goods and products are a liability until they are moved through the channels of distribution. Manufacturing, research, and development, warehousing, distribution—all are costs and liabilities until they are moved for consumption. In industry and business, nothing happens until somebody sells something.

"Like it or not, if you want to be successful and jump-start your career, learn the fundaments of how to communicate, how to sell and how to be a winner in dealing with people—that's what this course is all about."

If I could hitchhike on what the professor said, "That's what this *book* is all about."

If you are searching for a new career, a new start in life, to be your own boss, to be master and commander of your life and to write your own paycheck, this book will open new horizons for you. In these pages you will discover some basic advice as well as some advanced thinking about how to communicate and how to sell yourself and your ideas in a highly competitive world. Whatever your career path, whether it be building a business of your own, managing an office, winning a better job and making more money, or putting up with the pettiness and indifference of people, you must be able to communicate your thoughts with clarity to win compliance from others.

But first, be honest with yourself! What are the barriers keeping you from what you most desire in your life? What is it that keeps you from earning more money? Let me tell you what it is: It is your inability to communicate to and persuade others of the value of the skills and capabilities that you have to offer.

Properly directed, the power you have within you will give you the ability to "jump-start" your life. You can advance in your job, double or triple your income. Your ability, properly directed, will enable you to reach any goal you desire.

Every one of our industrial and business leaders, financial captains, intellectual leaders, and political statesmen and women started their careers with the mental capacity of the average individual.

They achieved their success by using their ability to communicate their opinions, their ideas, their perceptions, and their dreams of success to others.

The ability to communicate—the power to sell yourself and your ideas—is an acquired power. It is a talent that can be learned, practiced, and nurtured to enrich your career and your life.

In the pages of this book you will discover how you can become a skilled communicator to power-up your career and "jump-start" your life. Your success in life is contingent upon your ability to communicate and sell your value to others. Whatever your career choice—college professor, astronaut, doctor, lawyer or merchant—the ability to communicate and sell yourself is a prime requisite.

Introduction

One of the greatest discoveries in the history of the human species was when man awakened to learn he had the power to speak. This revelation spawned the birth of language and interpersonal communications.

The ability to speak, to use words to communicate thoughts, ideas, and benefits, is a power possessed only by humans. No other species—fish, fowl, insect, or animal—is blessed with the larynx and vocal cords that are essential to forming words and communicating.

Until that moment of revelation man communicated with others through paintings, body movements, and gestures Before man discovered that he was blessed with the talent to speak, the mouth was used for fighting, grubbing for food, and grunting audible sounds. (Some twenty-first century pessimists hold fast to the belief that the mouth is still used primarily for spewing out fighting and biting words, rather than communicating wisdom and good tidings.)

The discovery of language and the use of words to convey thoughts and ideas from one mind to another led to the discovery of salesmanship and to the ability to persuade others to accept new ideas and discoveries that would improve their lives.

H.G. Wells was adamant in his belief that man doesn't invent anything. His thesis was that for eons of time man was cold, naked and hungry, all the while standing over vast deposits of coal, food and fabric fibers just waiting to be discovered and used to improve the quality of life.

When asked if he was discouraged by so many failures in trying to invent the light bulb, Thomas Edison responded, "Not at all. I discovered 999 elements that wouldn't work." Edison didn't invent but, rather, discovered the light bulb—just like so many other so-called inventions that were really *discoveries*.

History is filled with stories of men and women who had the strength, the drive, the determination, the desire and the dedication to sell their ideas or their discoveries to a skeptical and wary public. Every facet of our lives has been touched by leaders who used their persuasive power to affect our lives for the better—in religion, science, government and the economics of daily life.

The United States of America enjoys freedom and liberty; we are a paragon of representative government to the rest of the world. This is our heritage, earned because of the dedication and persuasive sales power of George Washington, John Adams, Thomas Jefferson, Benjamin Franklin and a host of other great Americans with dreams for our nation.

Explorers, adventurers, and pioneers in science, industry and business followed these visionaries. Their ability to communicate and persuade others to accept their ideas, discoveries, and inventions led us to new heights in world leadership.

What are the forces that control human behavior? What affect do these forces have on the ability to communicate thoughts, ideas, and information? The answer to these questions impact all human relations—government, business, management, sales, marketing, advertising and interpersonal relationships.

How do you effectively communicate with others—friends, family, relatives, associates, customers, suppliers and employees? How do you communicate to be understood? How do you get compliance? How do you earn cooperation? How do you earn trust and loyalty and build solid relationships? Most important, how can you be sure people hear and understand what you say? It is important to be understood, but much more important that you are not *mis*understood.

The ability to communicate intelligently, in either the spoken or written word, is the magic key that opens the door to mutually beneficial relationships; it is the key to achieving agreement and creating harmony in our lives:

> In business, diplomacy and politics the ability to communicate and sell is the catalyst that turns managers into leaders and bottom lines into profit.

The human mind is a moving target that is subject to rapid and unexpected change. This means that as a communicator you must be verbally agile, quick on the draw, and fast on your feet to control the conversation and guide it to a satisfactory conclusion.

It is your job as a communicator to communicate. It is not the listener's responsibility to understand. As a communicator, you must realize that everyone to whom you speak is a uniquely different individual. If you want to be a winner, it is your responsibility to understand the needs, the desires, the values, the expectations, and the perceptions of each individual.

In society, as human beings, we expect from others the basic values of honesty, respect, diligence and morality. In return we expect to be listened to and receive a response to our needs.

The God-given talent to listen, when used to advantage, is your secret weapon as a communicator. This must be so, because you are blessed with two ears and one mouth, which is a signal that you should listen twice as much as you talk. Only by listening can your discover the inner feelings and desires of the person to whom you are speaking.

All communication should be a dialogue. The word dialogue is taken from the Greek words "dia" (flow) and "logue" (to speak). Winning communications should be interactive—a dialogue, a flow of meaningful information from one person to another.

But there is one major obstacle to overcome: conversation is conflict. On average, we speak at the rate of 125 words per minute, the brain can absorb 400 words per minute—but the brain can think at the rate of 1,000 words per minute.

This means that when you are talking your listener's mind is racing ahead of you shaping the response, rebuttal or reason why they don't want to do what you are asking them to do. As a communicator, it is your job to open the window of the listener's mind and to anchor thoughts there with rapier speed and effect. This focuses the mind and assures comprehension.

The forces that control human behavior are bound in words and psychology, reinforced with body language. Words paint pictures in the mind and psychology is the catalyst that triggers the action. In the pages of this book, I have revealed the not-too-secret secrets of effective communications and salesmanship that can make you a winner in your written or spoken transactions with people.

You can be a winner in dealing with people when you discover:

How to talk so people will want to listen to you.
How to listen so people will want to talk to you.

This is the essence of personal communications whether you are selling a product, a service, an idea, or yourself.

1 Everybody Does It

Having knowledge but lacking the power to express it clearly is no better than never having any ideas at all.

—Pericles, Greek, general and statesman

Every day you, and everyone you meet, are selling something. Stop to think how every day you have to sell yourself in or out of a situation:

- Talking your way out of a speeding ticket
- Asking your boss for a raise
- Teaching your children to avoid drugs, alcohol and cigarettes
- Urging your kids to study
- Telling salespeople why you can't buy today
- Getting others to do what you want them to do
- Winning arguments to your way of thinking
- Persuading your husband that you want to go out for dinner
- Convincing your wife you do not want to go out to dinner

Every waking hour you are faced with some situation that requires responsive selling techniques to be successful in your home, in your business, or in any social relationship with others. Every day of your life you are selling your opinion to others. In every conversation you are making an attempt to persuade someone to accept your viewpoint. Whether or not you recognize it, you are selling yourself to others.

To truly sell yourself to others, you must first find out their opinions, and opinions are tender points in the armor that people use to protect themselves. You find these tender points by asking questions. Once you know their tender point (opinion), you can persuade them to accept or to see things your way.

It's fairly easy to get your way in an argument or a discussion by sheer compulsion. You can bludgeon or bully someone into submission. There is an old adage that says, "A man convinced against his will is unconvinced still." There never is a winner in such an argument; both sides just harden in their opinions and, in the process, lose respect for each other.

Real winners lead by persuasion, not compulsion—this is the talent to encourage someone to do what you want them to do and to have them do it because they want to—and eagerly anticipate doing it.

Managers "require by compulsion," but Leaders "lead by gentle persuasion" with a touch of psychology and diplomacy. A fitting definition of diplomacy is the talent to tell someone to go to hell and to have him or her look forward to taking the trip.

Every hour of your day is spent talking—simply to converse and exchange greetings, to make a statement, to present or exchange ideas, to confess, to inform, to instruct, to inspire, to persuade, to gossip with neighbors over the backyard fence or just idle chatter.

Depending on the circumstances, the language used in conversation may be formal, informal, or colloquial. For example, precise, formal English would most likely be spoken in a high-level diplomatic meeting, while the language used in a relaxed business setting would be far more casual

But whatever form the language takes, the objective is always the same: to achieve a meeting of the minds. When the objective of the conversation is to convince or persuade someone to make up their mind or to change their mind, a working knowledge of psychology will make you a winner. Communications and sales skills are interrelated—both are essential to becoming a master communicator.

Ever look at the courses offered by university business schools? Lots of esoteric subjects, such as *Creating the Future, Nurturing Innovation, Strategic Thinking,* and *International Economics,* but very few on selling or salesmanship. They exist, but you have to work at it to find them. Maybe more important, I couldn't find a single course for non-business types on how to sell yourself or how to sell your ideas.

You may have the knowledge, skill and ability to perform, but if you cannot communicate with or convince others to accept your ideas, all is lost. Without communication skills and the ability to persuade others to lean your way, your brilliant ideas may never see the light of day. As a leader, you need to understand psychology and what it takes to persuade others to your way of thinking. It takes sales psychology and a mastery of words and a vivid imagination to be able to move people to accept innovative ideas in the marketplace. Your success in life is in direct relation to your ability to communicate and sell your abilities to others.

The missing ingredient in our educational institutions is the failure to teach students how to capitalize on their knowledge after acquiring it. In discussing this with two of my well-educated friends, both college professors—one a surgeon with an M.D. after his name and the other a respected scientist with a Ph.D. after his—expressed the same opinion. Doctors need to be educated in the winning techniques of a favorable bedside manner and the skill to maintain a meaningful dialogue with patients. Engineers and scientists need to know how to sell their ideas and innovations.

As my Ph.D. friend said, "Too many good ideas never see the light of day because of a failure to communicate. An example of how to overcome this hurdle is the way General Electric communicates its ideas in its advertising, "We make good things come to life" and "Imagination at work."

I recently interviewed a university graduate, an MBA. He was looking for a job. When I told him I had an opening for a salesman, he quickly replied, "Oh, I'm not interested in a sales job. I have a Masters Degree in Business Management." I replied, "Yes, I know, I just read your application. Is there something wrong with having a sales job?" Then he emphasized again, "I do have an MBA, and I believe my education warrants a management training position, not *just* a sales job."

Not once did he offer or try to persuade (i.e., *sell*) me as to *how* he could bring innovation, new ideas, and new marketing strategies to my company. I thought to myself: six years of theory, principles, and case studies, but not a single smidgeon devoted to how to sell his hard-earned knowledge. I'm sure this young man is going to go through life very disillusioned. That is, of course, unless he first learns how to sell himself and convince others of the value his abilities he can bring to their company.

Every corporation and institution is searching for men and women with innovative ideas and the skills to express their ideas with conviction and clarity to meet the challenges and the opportunities of the future. As I said earlier, nothing happens in this world until somebody sells something. Institutions of learning should offer more in-depth courses in communications and sales psychology to better prepare students to sell their skills and knowledge.

This is not a new idea. It dates back to 431 B.C., the time of the Peloponnesian War. Pericles, the ancient Greek statesman and general, had this to say about salesmanship and the power to communicate: "Having knowledge but lacking the power to express it clearly is no better than never having any ideas at all."

I have seen this scenario many times over. A person graduates from a university loaded with knowledge and degrees, but not an ounce of ability to carry on a convincing conversation. Then I have friends who barely made it through high school but radiate a personal charm when they walk into a room. Some people are born with this kind of charisma, others learn it. It is a talent that can be acquired with patience and practice.

Men and women of vision who forged our nation had the knowledge, the imagination and the sales skill to express it clearly. They had grand ideas and possessed the wisdom to know how to use the power of salesmanship to persuade others to share their dreams for a better life and to encourage the public to embrace their new ideas. They had to overcome lethargy, arcane opinions, and a reluctance to accept something new and different. They accomplished this through the power of salesmanship. The world is a better place because of this.

The innovative leader John Adams literally sold Congress on accepting the Declaration of Independence. Then he sold Great Britain on accepting the peace agreement. As ambassador to the Netherlands, he sold Holland on financing our new nation. Thomas Jefferson sold France the idea of investing in our new republic. Ben Franklin sold his discoveries and almanacs door-to-door before he, too, sold France on financing our new nation.

Later American leaders such as Andrew Carnegie, John D. Rockefeller, J.P. Morgan, John Jacob Astor, Cornelius Vanderbilt, and Henry

Ford brought us great railroads, steel mills, automobiles and financial institutions, People did not accept these new innovations willingly. Master communicators had to persuade people to see the benefits of their dreams.

Elisha Otis is just one extraordinary example. He put his life on the line to sell his discovery. Otis did not invent the elevator, but he did design a safety brake that made today's 100-story skyscrapers a reality. Primitive elevators were used primarily for moving materials in factories, mines, and warehouses. As people movers, they were considered too dangerous to risk life and limb riding them. Even with the assurance of Otis's safety brake, people refused to ride in them. They were content to walk up a flight of stairs. Because of this fear people had of accepting a new innovation, the height of buildings was limited to a few walk-up stories.

Otis had an idea how he was going to convince people of the safety of his power brake. His brake was installed on an elevator in a five-story building. He announced that he was going to personally ride the lift to the top of the building. Once there he would release the power and let the elevator go into a five-story free fall. At the appointed time a crowd gathered to watch Otis risk his life. When the elevator reached the top, Otis cut the power and it went into a free fall. To everyone's amazement, the brake worked.

This rather extreme "sales demonstration" was convincing. Sky scrapers with elevators are now a reality. Otis knew how to express his knowledge. Otis believed in himself and he believed in his product.

Gustavus Franklin Swift was the founder of the Swift meatpacking empire and the developer of the first icebox on wheels, better known as the refrigerator car. At the end of the Civil War, Chicago emerged as the railway hub for the distribution of livestock. Boxcars carried live cattle to all points of the nation, where the meat was butchered and marketed. Railroads thrived on the shipping volume, but Swift saw the waste of moving meat this way and developed a Reefer Car, or rolling icebox, to ship butchered and prepared meat safely, efficiently and at a lower cost to consumers.

Swift's idea was not popular with the railroads: Live cattle produced more revenue than processed meat. Swift was a salesman and he sold his idea of an icebox-on-wheels. His power to persuade and sell created more jobs and spawned many new distribution businesses to manage the marketing of refrigerated meat.

At the same time, while men were building industrial empires, dedicated and determined American women communicated the liberating message of freedom and equality for women with their winning civil, social and human rights movements.

Up until this point in time (the early 19th century), women's roll in life was confined to the kitchen and the bedroom; with a few exceptions women remained passive and silent allowing the men to take center stage in making history.

In the Civil war era and later, women found their voices and communicated their message well. No longer were they quiet and reserved; they stepped forward and made history-changing breakthroughs. They became powerful activists in education, politics and human rights.

Some of these resolute, compassionate and determined women were Susan B. Anthony, Amelia Bloomer, Ida B. Wells, Mary Edwards Walker, Elizabeth Cady Stanton and the unsinkable Molly Brown. All were master communicators who aggressively sold their breakthrough ideas to a skeptical and opinionated public.

Susan B. Anthony was a prominent civil rights leader. She played a prominent part in the 19th-century women's rights movement; she introduced women's suffrage into the United States. She was also an active participant in antislavery and temperance movements. Frederick Douglas, foremost leader in the abolitionist movement and President Lincoln's advisor during the Civil war, was a lifelong friend and associate of hers.

Elizabeth Cady Stanton and Amelia Bloomer, both leaders in the advancement of civil rights, were close friends and associates of Susan B. Anthony. These ladies joined together to form the first woman's temperance society of the United States. Amelia Bloomer is best remembered for her campaign to fight for freer dress for women, a campaign that she won (if Amelia could only see how her freer dress code has progressed into the 21st century). These three women became powerful public advocates of women's rights and stirring voices for change.

In one of her impassioned woman's rights speeches Anthony asked, "Where, under the Declaration of Independence, does the Saxon man get the power to deprive all women and Negroes of their inalienable rights?"

Ida B.Wells, African-American journalist and newspaper editor, was an inspirational leader for the civil rights. She was one of the most influential and inspiring black leaders of the time, along with Frederick Douglas. She was active in the civil rights and woman's suffrage movement. The organizations she founded later became the NAACP.

Wells was a fierce and tenacious competitor who communicated her convictions with persuasive force. She was a champion of those who didn't or couldn't speak up for themselves. In 1990, in her memory, the United States Postal Service issued a stamp in her honor.

Mary Edwards Walker is the only woman ever to receive the Congressional Medal of Honor. She was an American feminist, abolitionist, prohibitionist, alleged spy, prisoner of war and a surgeon. Walker was an independent-minded individualist. She often by her own desires wore men's clothing and on several occasions she was arrested for impersonating a man; this was her way of exercising her independence and equality.

She was one of the first women to graduate from a medical school, and at the beginning of the American civil war she served with the Union Army as the first-ever female U.S. Army Surgeon. She served on the front line of combat caring for the wounds of both Confederate and Union casualties. Captured by Confederate troops and arrested as a spy, Dr. Walker was imprisoned in Richmond, Virginia.

After the war, she became a writer and lecturer, supporting such issues as health care, temperance and women's rights. During World War II, a Liberty ship, The SS Mary Walker was named in her honor.

Margaret Brown is better known and remembered as "The Unsinkable Molly Brown." Maggie, as her friends called her, became an American socialite, philanthropist and activist.

She was a leader and a persuasive communicator. Molly Brown was aboard the Titanic the night it sunk. After helping other passengers into lifeboats she was finally persuaded to board the last boat to leave the stricken ship.

She became a hero this night by helping in the evacuation of the stricken ship. She even took an oar herself in the lifeboat. Molly garnered more fame as a great motivator and communicator when she persuaded the ship's crewman in charge of her boat to turn around and go back to rescue more survivors. To do this was much against his will and better judgment, fearing that his boat would be pulled down by the force of the Titanic's sinking; if not that, he was convinced that the force of people scrambling aboard would capsize the rescue boat.

Molly's forceful and commanding persuasion caused him to do as she directed. For her heroic effort, Margaret Brown was dubbed "The Unsinkable Molly Brown."

All these women had a passion for the causes they championed, reinforced with a firm resolve to be a winner. All entered active life with confidence in ordering and commanding to achieve their desired objective—of winning their way.

But they were wise enough to learn that there is a difference between acting on the principle of command and acting on the principle of common understanding. They learned that to be a winner in any crusade or conversation it is imperative to first get the viewpoint of the person or persons with whom you are communicating; then to reconcile it with your own as far as possible.

At every turn on the road to winning their crusade these women were opposed by men, and women too, who fiercely resisted changing the status quo and wanted to guard the past to prevent being thrust into the unproven future.

Through persistence and the power of meaningful communications their ideas were embraced–words were the bullets these strong-minded women used to win their campaign for social justice.

While men were building empires, dedicated and determined American women communicated the liberating message of freedom and equality. Because of the ideas championed by these Women's Rights crusaders, women will never be the same, neither will the free world.

These leaders were masters at communicating with and influencing others to believe in their vision. Today there is an urgent demand for leaders to match the masters of the past. There is a crying need in the social sciences, in the physical sciences, in politics, in government, in diplomacy and in all the relationships of daily personal and business life for *master communicators*: people who want the excitement of bringing new ideas and innovations to life.

If you are like many men and women, young and old, who are driven to build a fulfilling career, to be leaders, to rise above the ordinary and to enjoy the personal satisfaction of outstanding accomplishment, a career as a *master communicator* will catapult you to dazzling heights. You will be your own boss, you can write your own ticket to success, your skills will be in great demand and great shall be your financial and personal reward.

Master communicators have learned how to use the power of words to write, to speak, and to communicate with gentle persuasion. Queen Victoria, the British monarch, once was asked, "Why is Prime Minister Benjamin Disraeli your favorite? And why do you not like Prime Minister William Gladstone?" Her reply was, "When Gladstone speaks to me it is like he is addressing an audience, but Prime Minister Disraeli, he speaks to me like I am a woman." Disraeli was a salesman, a master communicator who knew his audience and in his conversation catered to its whims.

It is time to awaken the sleeping giant in you called salesmanship. It is time for you to become a master communicator—and to have *fun* doing it too. You will discover the personal inner strength to achieve mastery of yourself and the power to make you a winner in every facet of your life. Absolutely nothing happens in the world until somebody sells something. Whatever your education or profession, become a master communicator and make good things happen for you.

2 Master Communicators

Nothing happens in business until someone sells an idea, a product or a service.

Shirl, Elliott & Frank. No, this is not a law firm or an ad agency. These three guys in their heyday of vigor, health and wealth were called hawkers, peddlers, drummers, traders and itinerants. Each one made a good living each month. This was during the Depression years of the 1930s when bread lines and soup kitchens fed the hungry and unemployed. Seldom, if ever, would you see a salesman in the line.

They didn't mind being called hawkers. They made money and laughed all the way to the bank. They were "salesmen" and proud to claim the title. Meeting and learning from these three communicators and salesmen was the rudder that steered me safely through the shoals of my early life.

Becoming a salesman was an obsession with me. Raised during the Depression years, I witnessed people in all walks of life struggling for existence. I saw professional men and women bartering their talents and degrading their skills for food, clothing, and shelter.

I was old enough to observe one fact that changed the course of my life: Plumbers, plasterers, carpenters and bricklayers fared much better than some professionals who were forced into unskilled labor jobs.

One other skill fed my imagination. Salespeople, men and women with the skill to convince and persuade, always appeared to me to be better off than others. The *Los Angeles Times* newspaper where I worked had a sales staff of 50 street salesmen and another 50 sales-women and 25 salesmen who worked on the telephone. Everyone was on a commission, and their paycheck reflected their success as sales-people. Some succeeded, others failed. I knew a few who were earning as much as $100 a week, and I was convinced selling was for me.

Every business was desperate for sales and searching for sales men and women willing to work on a commission basis. In an article published in one of its sales newsletters, Dartnell reported the following:

> During the Depression years when only 55 percent to 61 percent of the work force was employed, 75 percent of people who were salespeople were working and earning 50 percent more than other workers.

This observation set my career choice in concrete. I wanted to be a professional salesman, which later morphed into becoming a master communicator, in both the written and the spoken word.

As I recall the Great Depression Years it brings to mind our current economic situation. In 2010 we are faced with problems reminiscent of the 1930s; we are in an economic situation bordering on depression and runaway inflation, there is double-digit unemployment and fear for the future.

Today there is a great proliferation of desirable products, but there is a shortage of customers willing to spend money in these uncertain times. It was the same in the 1930s; people needed their confidence restored and master communicators with the power to persuade paved the road to recovery. The same is true today, we need master communicators with new ideas to open the door to the future.

The first few sales-communication jobs I had scared me to death. I almost threw in the towel and gave up selling as a career.

But then I met Shirl, who was a telemarketing salesman for the *Los Angeles Times*. He took this neophyte under his wing and opened new horizons to me. He talked about words and how to use them and the elements of psychology that touch emotions and spark sales.

Now let me introduce you to Shirl.

Shirl was a broad-shouldered, powerful man, but he was crippled from the waist down. His legs were crutches, but he was blessed with a deep, mellow, and vibrant voice that could charm the gold right out of your teeth. He used his voice to make money. He was a salesman. His office was an easy chair, a desk, and a telephone that connected him to his marketplace. And he knew and practiced the power of words to close sales.

His real name was Shirley. Now how could a man live having a girl's name? First of all, he didn't. He shortened it to Shirl. The finest tailored suits and impeccable haberdashery were his standard. He was a master communicator, a direct salesman who made weekly trips to the bank to deposit the commissions and bonuses he earned selling.

I was an eighteen-year-old kid easily impressed by successful people who were earning big bucks. I listened to Shirl's sales spiel. It was not brash or bragging. The tone, cadence, and rhythm of his voice plus his mastery of words elicited trust and confidence. I was smitten by his winning ways. Now there was no doubt in my mind, I wanted to be a salesman and make as much money as he did. I will come back to Shirl later.

Now I want to introduce you to Elliott.

When I first met Elliott, he was in his late seventies. He had capped off a successful and financially rewarding career as a salesman, sales trainer, manager, teacher, and speaker. During his business life and as a young man he rubbed elbows with sales greats like Dale Carnegie who, in 1935, authored the book *How to Win Friends and Influence People*. The book became an instant success and made the bestsellers list. Today, in the twenty-first century, Carnegie's book is still one of the bestsellers in bookstores and on the Internet. People are still clambering for a book that was written in 1935. It is a fact of life, from the beginning of time: People want to have friends and be a friend, they want to love and be loved, and they want to be a winner in dealing with each other.

To show you what the power of words can do, when Dale Carnegie's book was first published two titles were tested. The pages in the book were the same, word for word. The two titles were *How to Ruin Your Marriage in the Quickest Possible Way* and *How to Win Friends and Influence People*. The first title failed because it attracted people who wanted a book about marriage, not about how to win friends. Words are powerful persuaders when arranged in the right way.

People haven't changed. Human nature is constant. In every respect it is the same today as it was in the days of King Tut: People still have a burning desire to make friends and to be successful. A quote attributed to William James, an American philosopher and psychologist, puts it cogently: "Man's innermost desire is to be recognized as an individual; everyone wants to be appreciated and loved."

One of the sales greats with whom Elliott associated was Elmer Wheeler. He coined the phrase, "Don't Sell the Steak, Sell the Sizzle." By selling the "sizzle" he meant selling the benefits the product delivers. Another mentor of Elliott's was John Patterson, founder and president of the National Cash Register Company, better known today as NCR. He manufactured and produced an innovative product called a cash register. His was an era of discovery and innovation.

During this same time Edison developed the light bulb, Burroughs the adding machine, Bell the telephone, and Sholes the typewriter (which was manufactured and sold under the name of Remington). This era could well mark the birth of modern marketing and modern communications. These innovations signaled the need for professional communicators and salespeople. Products are a financial liability and a capital cost for manufacturers until someone sells it and someone buys it.

This was the major problem that Patterson faced with his new cash register: There was no demand for cash registers and therefore no market. Patterson knew he had a product that would solve a string of problems, such as theft, pilfering, and undocumented losses, that plagued many businesses.

Business executives struggled to find better methods of tracking and managing inventory and sales. NCR salespeople communicated the good word and demonstrated how this new innovation would improve financial management and transfer more profit to the bottom line. Patterson knew he had a product whose time had come. He also knew that in order to make a profit, products had to be moved and to move products, you had to move people to buy. He needed salesmanship, so he "invented" it.

Around 1895, Patterson introduced professional salesmanship. This concept lifted the Yankee Peddler, Hawker, and Drummer from "Pitchman" to the status of Professional Salesperson. Patterson pioneered the concept of training salespeople to be professionals. He trained his sales staff in product features but more importantly, the staff was trained to sell the *benefits* the customer would enjoy from the product. Patterson initiated the idea, *"sell solutions, not products."* People are only interested in what job the product will do for them; all they want to know is, **What's In It For Me?** So, sell benefits and show the features that make the benefits possible.

There is a little poem that gets to the heart of selling benefits. It was written by a mail order icon named Victor O. Schwab.

Tell Me Quick and Tell Me True

I see that you've spent a big chunk of dough
To tell me things you think I should know.
That your plant is so fine, so big and so strong
That your founder had whiskers so handsome and long.

So your firm started business back in old '92
How awfully in'tresting that might be—to you!
That the boss built the business with the blood of his life.
(Oh! Gee! I'll run home and tell that to my wife!)

Your machinery is modern and oh! —so complete—
Your reputation flawless—your workers so neat.
And your motto is "Quality" with a capital "Q"
(I'm getting fed up with that stuff about "You"!)

Will it save me money, or time or work?
Or hike my pay with a welcome jerk?
What drudgery, worry or loss will it cut?
Can it yank me out of a personal rut?

Perhaps it can make my appearance so swell
That telephone calls will wear out the bell
And thus I might win me a lot of new friends
(And one never knows where such a thing ends)!

I wonder how much it will do for my health?
Could it show me a way to acquire some wealth?
Better things for myself, for the kids, and my wife?
Or how to quit work somewhat early in life?

So Tell me Quick and Tell me True
Or else my love—to H—with you!
Say less about how your product came to be
And more what the darned stuff DOES FOR ME!

Patterson was a sales visionary and a hard taskmaster. He was slow to hire, but quick to fire anyone who did not comply with his systematic approach to selling. He was also one of the first managers to reward sales performance with incentive bonuses. Patterson developed sales presentations into a fine art and raised the standards of selling from the vaudeville tactics of carnival barkers into a vital and respected part of American business management.

The annals of American business and industry are filled with the names of leaders who learned their sales skills under the capable direction of NCR's John Patterson. Thomas Watson of IBM; Henry Ford; Charles Kettering and R. Grant of General Motors; and Bill Benton, founder of the famed advertising agency Benton & Bowles (and later a U.S. Senator)—this is just a sampling of the leaders who trained under and applied Patterson's principles and psychology of selling to their businesses.

NCR's systemized method of selling was also based on the work of Arthur Frederick Sheldon. Sheldon classified the principles of selling into a scientific framework. One of his outstanding contributions was outlining the steps that are essential in every sale:

Favorable attention ripens into interest which, when held, arouses desire and culminates into decision and action.

Sheldon and Patterson were the real founders of professional salesmanship.

Sheldon had another definition of selling. His alliterative "6 Ps" still stands as the best all time definition of salesmanship. He pictured salesmanship as six peas in a pod:

The **POWER** to **PERSUADE PEOPLE** to **PURCHASE** a **PRODUCT** at a **PROFIT**

Elliott was a product of this generation. He practiced professional salesmanship, he trained sales staffs, and he taught the principles of professional salesmanship. In talking to Elliott, he said, "Patterson, Wheeler and Carnegie are all icons of modern salesmanship. They were master communicators, and I honed my skills from their examples, plus I added a few of my own."

Elliott had hired, trained, and coached sales staffs in many lines of business and under highly competitive situations. There was no fading of the light in this man's life. He was still energetic, filled with the juice of life and looking for new sales challenges. I managed to keep him well occupied.

I hired him as a sales consultant and sales writer. At the time, I was a partner in a direct marketing agency. I was fresh out of the Marine Corps, thirty years old with a fire in my belly to build a business and make money. Journalism was my vocation, but salesmanship was my passion. I wanted to hone my skills in selling and I hoped that in working with Elliott his sales savvy would rub off on me.

Elliott was a master persuader. Sure, he was a salesman, but he claimed his success was being *a Purchase Advisor to customers and a Business Builder to the people for whom he worked.* He called this an attitude adjustment to redirect his vocation.

When Elliott was a young boy, a fire changed his life forever. It was, in fact, the catalyst that led him to become a star salesman. I'll tell you this story later when I share his sales secrets with you.

To finish off my list of super motivators, let me introduce you to Frank.

During the Roaring Twenties, in the heyday of Prohibition, jazz, and the introduction of the new dance craze called the Charleston, Frank sold pianos door-to-door. Imagine if you can an itinerant peddler going door-to-door selling pianos. "Impossible," you say. "How does he carry the samples?" You might imagine Frank as being a glib, fast-talking carnival pitchman. You might picture him in a gaudy suit and tie, slick-backed hair and a cigar clenched in his teeth.

The image of a salesman was personified by the handsome Professor Harold Hill in *The Music Man.* The professor sold musical instruments and mesmerized an entire town with promises of the glory and the salvation music would bring to the children. He contrasted those benefits to the evils of the game of pool, spelled with a capital "P," that could only lead to trouble with a capital "T."

Frank was the antithesis of this stereotype. He was short and on the roly-poly side of portly. The sparse plumage on his head had seen better days. His face was best described as "cherubic," and it exuded trust and confidence. Frank had a chuckle that was infectious—to hear it, you would say it sparkled to match the twinkle in his eye—particularly when he was winning a sale.

I wanted to pick Frank's brain to discover the secrets that made him a master persuader. To get Frank, I bought his office supply business and put him on the street. I would tag along on these calls with the hope of discovering the magic elixir of selling. I was confused; there was not a winning formula. He didn't use "power words" to close a sale.

One trait differentiated Frank from the pack of sales persuaders roaming the streets in search of sales:

Frank listened. He didn't say much, but he asked questions and listened. Armed with the information of what people wanted, Frank sold solutions to their problems.

Other salesmen's heads were filled with all the old hard-sell phrases: "Go for the Jugular; Selling begins when the prospect says NO; Your job is to sell—give 'em hell." etc., etc. Sales training and sales rallies filled their minds with show-no-mercy aggression. It was sell or else. Untrained salespeople sold products!!!—not Solutions to Problems—and never achieved their full potential. Also, these types of selling tactics fostered an unsavory association with the title "salesman."

Canny, shrewd-thinking Frank had learned that *to know* the problem that needed a solution was the key to sales success. He asked questions. He listened. He understood the customer's problem and he made certain the customer understood his solution. Frank delivered solutions. He sold products. He made very good money.

I'll divulge his secrets to you in later chapters.

3 Using Words to Communicate

Nothing is as important as saying the right thing in the right amount at the right time to the right people.

—Plato

Shirl had a knack for saying the right thing in the right amount at the right time to the right people. He was skilled in the use of words to communicate and to be understood.

My longing for a pair of track shoes led to my introduction to Shirl.

I really didn't *need* them, but I desperately *wanted* them. The kind of shoes with spikes in them that would propel me like a sixty-mile-per hour cheetah in Saturday's track meet.

So what does a fifteen-year-old boy do? You're right. I asked my Dad for $1.65 so I could buy my track shoes. Pop reminded me that there was a critical depression on and that jobs and money were scarce. He suggested I find a job and earn the money to buy my shoes.

Down but determined, I canvassed the local businesses. The owner of a garage and gas station offered to pay me a dollar if I would sand and ready a 1929 Model A Ford Roadster for a paint job. I took the job, and after twelve hours of solid muscle work my boss was so delighted that he not only paid me the dollar, he offered me ten dollars a week to pump gas in his service station. To a fifteen-year-old high school student, ten dollars a week was a fortune. I already had a job delivering newspapers, so I worked out a timetable to accommodate both jobs.

I opened the gas station at 7:00 A.M. From 9:00 A.M. to 3:00 P.M., I attended school. After school I delivered my newspapers. From 5:00 P.M. to 7:00 P.M., I pumped gas. Then it was home to dinner and study.

This was about the time the singing commercial, or "jingle," was first appearing on the radio (television was yet to be invented). The gas station where I worked sold Gilmore Blu-Green gas; the blue-green (aka, blugreen) color gave the product a unique point of difference from competing gasolines.

Gilmore's advertising "Jingle" was a winner. Hear it once and you were humming it the rest of the day. It captured my mind and I can still, seventy-eight years later, remember the tune. Here it is:

Blu-Green Gas. Blu-Green Gas. Use it in your motor and be full of class. There's no one on the highway you can't pass, unless they're using Blu-Green, too.

Gilmore also used the flying ace and legend Roscoe Turner to capture the minds of the consumers. Turner used to fly in his plane carrying a real live lion as a co pilot. The lion's name was "Gilmore," of course.

This was pure showmanship combined with salesmanship. It was my first and most compelling lesson in the power of moving people to action. Right then and there I set in concrete my dream of becoming a communicator specializing in advertising.

Gilmore built a business that was sold to Mobil Oil, whose identifying icon was the flying horse Pegasus. Now I was pumping Mobil gas. The company initiated a contest to see which salesperson could sell the most of a new product called Upperlube, a gasoline additive that would help improve miles-per-gallon gas consumption or save a gallon of gas in every tankful.

I won the contest. I sold the most Upperlube, but my gas sales went down. Every time a customer came in, I sold a ten-cent can of Upperlube. Here's how I did it. Gas was twelve cents a gallon, Upperlube ten cents. I told customers to buy the Upperlube and reduce their gas purchase by one gallon—and in the process save two cents.

Finally the boss called me into his office and explained my job was to sell the additive in addition to the gas. This was the tipping point that forged my career. I became a disciple of the power of the written and spoken word to make me a winner in my daily verbal intercourse with people.

One of my customers at the gas station was a salesman. I knew he was successful because he drove a beautiful new car and dressed like he had just stepped off a page of *Esquire* magazine. I asked him what I should do to make money and be a winner. His sage advice was, "Son, learn about life. Understand and learn what motivates people." Then he added, " College would be good for you, but to really see life in all its many facets, visit circuses, carnivals and religious revivals. There you'll get a gutty cross-section of life and learn what motivates people, be they paupers or princes. You will discover that every person likes to be entertained. People enjoy being fooled—not too much—just a little bit, as long as it evokes a chuckle but doesn't harm them."

This is when I began to attend carnivals, circuses and revivals. It became a passion of mine. To this day I still get great joy and inspiration from watching and listening to men and women who have a way with words selling their wares on television or on street corners. This is still a great education in using the power of words to be a winner in dealing with people. It is also a lesson in separating the fake from the genuine, the truths from the lies, the right way to influence and the wrong way to influence the action of others.

I was almost a high school dropout, but I did manage to graduate. Higher education was out of the question. I didn't have the money, and I thought I had learned just about everything there was to learn. It was time to be a full-time member of the work force, to get a job and make some money.

I discovered that finding a job was not easy. I heard the *L.A. Times* might be hiring in the advertising department, so I headed for the city. When I arrived, there was a line of well over twenty jobless people anxious to be picked for the available job. I didn't make it. Every day for the next three weeks, I made the trek to the *Times*, praying there would be an opening.

Finally, one morning I hit pay dirt. Standing with a group of other hungry hopefuls, I was singled out. The hiring boss, as I called him, pointed straight at me and said, "Boy, take this ad proof down to Mary O'Brien at the Broadway and get it okayed." Then he added, "Make it snappy. There's a deadline in just 45 minutes."

I knew where the Broadway department store was located, at

Fourth and Broadway, but I didn't know Mary O'Brien. I grabbed the advertisement and took off running. Four blocks later, out of breath, I ran into the store and asked an official-looking sales clerk, "Where would I find a Mary O'Brien?" "Fourth floor," he directed. Off I went, got the proof okayed and reported back to the *Times*.

As the proof was delivered, the Boss looked quizzically at me over his horn-rimmed glasses and asked, "Who are you? Do you work here?" I gave him my best smile and replied, "I don't, but I hope I do now." He laughed and told me that he'd seen so much of me the last few weeks, he assumed I was an employee. Then he snapped, "Well, dammit, get that silly grin off your face, take off your coat and go to work. You're hired."

I wasn't hired as a salesman, but I had learned my first magic word: Persistence: Keep at it, never give up.

I remember reading a quotation by President Calvin Coolidge. He was affectionately known as Silent Cal. He was soft-spoken and an accomplished public speaker. He was noted for his economy in the use of words when making a point. "Stingy" best describes his use of words, but he said a mouthful with this pronouncement about the power of persistence:

> Persistence—Press on:
> —Nothing in the world can take the place of Persistence.
> Talent will not:
> —Nothing is more common than unsuccessful men or women with talent.
> Genius will not:
> —Unrewarded genius is almost a proverb.
> Education alone will not:
> —The world is full of educated derelicts.
> Persistence and Determination are Omnipotent!

Silent Cal was right; persistence rewarded me with a job at the *Times*. I landed in the classified advertising department.

The dispatch desk in the classified department was my first "real" job. It was here that I first met Shirl and where I learned to write a nineteen-word ad for an apartment for rent in just two agate lines:

1 brm apt 3rd fl fr esc ldry rm no
pts bs stp 1 blk $4wk call1234

Obviously this was in the "pre-Twitter" days, but the need for economy of words was just as necessary. I learned how to use words sparingly and how to make every word count. After the early edition of the newspaper was put to bed it was 9:00 P.M. I didn't go home. I moved over to Shirl's desk for my sales training lesson.

His first comment was, "Bob, before you can sell, you have to have a product. Then you have to find a market that has a problem your product can solve."

This made good sense to me, so I asked, "Shirl, I know I have the product. It's the classified ad section of the *Times*. But, who is my market?" He pointed to a broom in the corner of the room and told me:

See all those 3" x 5" pink pieces of paper on the floor? Take that broom and sweep them together. You'll notice to each slip of paper is pasted a classified ad from one of the other seven competing newspapers in Los Angeles. The salesmen who tossed them on the floor didn't take time to call and make a sale.

These people all have apartments, rooms, and houses for rent. They need the money from the rentals to make payments on their mortgages. Stack these "sales leads" neatly in front of your telephone. You now have a market of people who need what you have to sell. Start selling.

"Wow," I thought to myself, "this is easy. Now I'm ready to sell and make money."

"Not so fast" counseled Shirl. "First, you have to prepare and rehearse your sales pitch. Tell people who you are. Explain your product. Show the benefit to them. Then ask for the order."

"Piece of cake," I said, as I strapped on the telephone headset to make my first foray into sales. I had my spiel down pat and had selected the nom de plume of Bob Kelly. Hemmings was too long and I figured a familiar, friendly name like Kelly would exude trust and self-assurance.

With confidence, I dialed the first rooms-for-rent leads. It was now

11:00 P.M. When the rooming house manager sleepily answered the phone, I blurted out:

> Good evening, madam, my name is Bob Kelly of the *Los Angeles Times*. I see you have rooms for rent. Would you like to place a classified ad in the *Times* tomorrow and rent some of those rooms? It will only cost you five dollars to put your name in front of 400,000 people for four days.

Then I waited for an answer. On the first five sales pitches I was rewarded with:

> Two hang-ups. One 'Go to hell.' One 'Shove it.' One blistering burst of profanity for getting her out of bed at 'this ungodly hour.'

Little did I know how on target I was in calling some rooming house managers "Madam." A few were "practicing" madams and wasted no words in bartering their services in exchange for an ad in the *Times*. At the tender age of seventeen it was my indoctrination into life in the big city.

I was learning. Shirl watched and listened and noted my reaction to five "rejects" and no sales. "Lesson number one," he said, "when someone answers the phone and says, 'Hello,' you have to overcome four basic obstacles standing in your way to making a sale:

1. They don't need what you have to sell.
2. They don't have the desire to buy.
3. They don't have the money.
4. They don't like or trust you.

"As a salesman, you must overcome these obstacles. In time, selling will teach you to be a perennial optimist. Always think positively. Rejections are only challenges for you to improve your skills. Put positive thoughts and optimistic feelings in your mind. Always maximize the positive and minimize the negative. Eventually you will gain confidence and assurance that many people will buy from you because you are delivering money- saving or time-saving benefits to them.

"To do this," he continued, "you must sharpen your sales talk. You have to learn how to transfer *Selling Points* to *Buying Points*. Sales points are what your product is; buying points are what your product will do for the buyer. All your prospect wants to know is:

What Will This Product or Service Do For Me?"

With this advice, I rewrote my sales pitch and tested it on the next five cold calls. I began by saying, "Good evening, madam, my name is Bob Kelly. As you know, money is hard to come by today."

I was saying something with which she was familiar. Money was almost impossible to come by in these hard times. She was agreeing with me, nodding "Yes." Getting agreement is the first step to making a sale.

Then I followed with, "I have an idea for you that will put money in the bank for you so you can pay off your mortgage and put food on your table."

This triggered an emotion.

Then came the solution: "Let me put a $2.50 classified ad in the *Times* for you, then 400,000 people will see it and you only need one caller to rent your room. Don't you agree this would be a worthwhile investment?"

With these new *buying points*, my sales hit pay dirt. After five more cold calls, I received:

- Two sales
- Two hang-ups
- One command punctuated with profanity

By two in the morning I finished calling my stack of sales leads. Flush from the thrill of success, I counted ten sales, fifteen hang-ups, ten call-back-laters, and three new insights on profanity to add to my vocabulary.

The real thrill was the revelation that through selling I was personally benefiting by helping people enjoy a better life. I was giving them hope of renting their rooms and making money to pay their bills and put food on their tables. "God," I thought to myself, "selling is the best damned job in the world. It's not work; I'm bringing joy and comfort to everyone I sell."

This epiphany focused a new light on my perception of salesmanship. When I made a sales call, I was not an interruption in someone's life. It was a pleasant interlude because I delivered a solution to a problem.

It was exciting to think that my sales skills had brought joy to ten people, even though I had awakened them at two in the morning. Some people are wonderful, and others just had no use for what I was offering—like the ones who didn't buy from me. No harm done, just no sale.

Shirl knew that he had opened my mind to a career in sales that night. Several nights each week I would seek his advice and he generously shared his time and talent. He filled my mind with the power of words and the psychology to motivate people to action.

Some points were personal to him. He told me, "As a handicapped person, I am bound to a desk and a telephone. I don't have the advantage of meeting customers face to face so I can see their body language, their facial responses. Without any physical contact, I am forced to learn how to use the magic power of words to extend my personality over the telephone."

He demonstrated the power of words as I listened to him make his telephone sales calls. He used single syllable words—short, "fuzzy" words—that were comforting, easily understood, and made the journey from his mind to the listener's mind without a hiccup or an interruption of thought. His point was that the one major hurdle to communication of thoughts is that people don't necessarily hear what you think you said. "Just remember, it isn't what you say or what you mean, it's what the other person believes or understands you said."

The best advice he gave me to hone my skills to a fine edge was to get Newton's book on physics. Then he suggested I commit to memory Newton's laws of motion. I had been exposed to them in high school but had paid them little attention. If I was interested in winning an argument, making a point, selling an idea, proposition or product, he said, Newton had some sound advice for me. Then he suggested I commit these laws to memory:

Law 1. Inertia—A body at rest will so continue until acted upon by some outside force. A body will stay inert until some force moves it and gets it off dead center.

Law 2. Acceleration—A body will accelerate in the direction the force is applied.

Law 3. Recoil—For every action there is an opposite and opposing action (action is equal to reaction).

Shirl asked whether or not I understood Newton's laws. I told him that I did, but didn't see how they applied to sales. He was ready with the answer:

> A prospect is not anxiously waiting for you to call. This is *Inertia*. As a salesman your job is to say something of substance that will grab his attention, such as, 'I have an idea for you that will make you money or save you money.' This is *Acceleration*. Then comes *Recoil (or Reaction)*—all the reasons or excuses he has to avoid buying from you. Your job is to overcome the recoil.

Then he went on to what he called *sales attitude*. He gave me his FUN-damentals of being a salesman:

> Notice the word 'FUN.' Selling is a game, a FUN game in which you match wits with your prospect. Every sales call is a challenge to test your skill with words and ideas to win the mind of your prospect. Vince Lombardi, coach of the Green Bay Packers, summed up winning when he said, "Winning isn't everything, it's the only thing."
>
> The FUN is when you make a sale. Both the seller and the buyer are winners. Your buyer has traded his money for something that will deliver greater benefits than the money he paid, and you win, too, when you carry your money to the bank. Sell and grow Rich and have fun doing it."

He was right.

Shirl's tutelage had many facets. He exposed me to the bad in selling as well as the good, and he taught me the difference. He pointed out the sloppy sales techniques of hacks, salespeople who hit and run, using intimidation and ploys to make a sale. Selling's prime purpose, he counseled, is to acquire customers, then to develop them into loyal customers who will continue to purchase products and services offered by you.

> People buy from you for two reasons: (1) they like you, and (2) they like your sales proposition.

"Your first and foremost job in selling," he said "is to make people like you." And he told me about a famous trial lawyer who claimed that the goal of his first presentation to the jury was to make them like his client. Even though they find the defendant guilty, if the jury liked him, they would be more lenient in their verdict.

During this time, but after I met Shirl, the paper hired a sales consultant named Paul Ivey to conduct a series of sale training courses. A top sales executive, Ivey was noted for his famous "Hammer" story. In it he described the amateur salesman selling the hammer. He would say in a slovenly and uninspired way, "A hammer's a hammer. It's a good tool. If you need to pound in nails or pull them out, this will do the job."

Ivey said there is inherent drama in every product that lifts it out of the ordinary. And then he told how a sales professional would sell a hammer:

This is more than just a hammer. It is a finely made precision tool that will make it easy for you to do your carpentry work. The hammerhead is forged from tempered steel for durability. The nail-pulling claws are arched at a 45-degree angle to give added leverage for easy nail extraction. The handle is made of aged hickory shaped to fit the contour of your hand and relieve muscle stress. The hickory handle is sweat into the head and reinforced with steel brads to give you the assurance the handle will not separate from the head even under extreme use.

When I found that Paul Ivey was teaching salesmanship at the University of Southern California, I decided to go to USC and earn a college degree. I applied, was accepted, and registered as a freshman.

Then came the moment of truth. I was earning $50 a month at the *L.A. Times*. At the cashier's window I was informed the fee for the fall semester was $165. Oops, I forgot. Education costs money. I discovered you pay for the *learning* years. When you graduate and find a job these are the *earning* years. Finally, to finish the scenario of a successful career, you enjoy the retirement and the *payoff* years.

My sole asset was the pride of my life—a polished and chromed Studebaker convertible coupe called the Rockne, after the famous Notre Dame football coach Knute Rockne.

It was one of the top-quality automobiles of the day, The car was a beauty, and it had power.

For me, it was decision time: college or my beautiful Rockne convertible with its green leather upholstery, jumbo air wheels, and radio. College won. I sold the car for $250, paid the $165 to USC, bought $30 worth of books, and spent $40 for a suit, two pairs of slacks, a sport coat, shoes, and accessories. Oh, yes, I had to pay a $10 commission to the salesman who introduced me to the man who bought my car. I kept $5 for spending money.

Advertising and selling was my passion and the *Los Angeles Times* newspaper offered me a job in the classified advertising department to fit my school schedule.

I spent any free time I had on South Spring Street listening to pitchmen selling their wares—spark rejuvenators for automobiles, kitchen utensils, and medical elixirs guaranteed to cure everything internally and externally from dandruff to athlete's foot. They were fast on their feet and glib with words. They would gather a crowd by promising miracle sexual fulfillment, relief from heartburn, bad teeth, ailing eyesight, and other life-threatening problems. They kept their audience spellbound with their stinging verbal warnings and promises. Their vocabulary was redolent with self-interest words like *Revolutionary, Never before offered, Amazing, Sensational, Secret Formula,* and others designed to stir the imagination and generate the desire to hear more.

One pitchman pitched a medical elixir guaranteed to stop the aging process. In a sizzling delivery, he promised that his elixir would cure everything—"whatever ails you." I was tremendously impressed by his sales and speaking skills. He had a way with words and a delivery that mesmerized the gathering crowd. I would loiter around on the fringe of the crowd, watching and listening, as he made his pitch. He noticed my regular presence and offered me fifty cents to stand close to him holding a bottle of the juice and to attest to the accuracy of his promise should anyone question his integrity.

He would end his presentation with, "I personally use this and I am eighty-five years old (he looked to be in his thirties)." Once in a while a listener would sidle up to me and ask, "Hey, kid, is he really eighty-five?" Looking my eighteen years, I would reply, "I don't honestly know, sir. I have only been with him twenty-five years."

Sundays would find me attending religious revivals at Washington and Figueroa boulevards, where one of many and sundry evangelists were preaching salvation. Another hangout for me was the Four Square Gospel Church in Echo Park, California, where a dynamic woman minister named Aimee Semple McPherson mesmerized her audience with hellfire-and-damnation healing sermons.

Sister Aimee as she was called became one of the most charismatic and influential persons of her time. She was a folk hero, a civic institution and a patron saint of service clubs. Sister Aimee pioneered the use of modern media especially radio. This was the dawn of the commercial radio industry. Radio programming was sparse and people would gather around their radios to marvel at this new discovery that let them listen to people talking many miles away.

Sister Aimee took advantage of this new phenomenon called radio; nightly thousands of people would gather around their radios to listen to her sermons. Her church, The International Church of the Foursquare Gospel, had a seating capacity of 5,300 people which she filled to capacity three times a day Seven days a week.

Her power with words wove magic in her listeners' minds. Her healing sermons would mesmerize mentally and spiritually handicapped people persuading them to throw away their crutches and to forget their impediments. Some did as she asked and walked away. Not once did I ever see anyone fall flat on his or her face. She was a persuader. She separated people from their fears and their anxieties. She also separated them from a lot of their money.

My interest in attending these services was not for personal salvation. I was a college student doing my homework and looking for inspiration. My imagination was captured by the power this woman had to capture such an attentive audience.

I was moved and hypnotized by her fire-and-brimstone sermons and by the sincerity with which she delivered her message. Her presentations were rich in the use of dynamic words that painted vivid pictures on the canvas of my mind.

Barnum & Bailey and the Ringling Brothers circuses were also a magnet to me. Every time either circus came to town, I was in attendance. I liked to watch the acrobats, the clowns, and the animal acts, but I spent the lion's share of my time traveling up, down, and around the midway. I was spellbound by the fast-talking, persuasive carnival barkers as they pulled in the audience to see the Bearded Lady, Dolly

Dimple the fattest girl in the world, the Siamese Twins, the Sword Sallower, the Flame Eater, the Escape Artist, Lionel the Lion-Faced Boy, and other Freaks and Monstrosities of Nature—plus, always, a bevy of belly and hootchy-kootchy dancers.

As I watched these unusual souls expose themselves and sacrifice their dignity to earn a living, I asked myself, what is the magnet that attracts people to want to see these misfits of society?

The author George Orwell gave me the answer in his book *Politics and the English Language:* "If I wanted to get myself noticed, I would stand on my head instead of standing upright." People are attracted by the unusual, the out-of-the-ordinary. Every individual has a unique point of difference. This uniqueness might be genetic or acquired. Either way, it's a necessary ingredient.

Successful people capitalize on any unusual aspects of their physical appearance or persona. The old-time song-and-dance man Jimmy Durante is a good example. His prominent proboscis protruding from his face propelled him to fame and fortune. Babe Ruth was known for his booming bat that hit record-breaking home runs. Winston Churchill lifted himself above the crowd with his mastery of the English language. George Burns is forever linked to his omnipresent cigar. It is not just the misfits that attract others. People are attracted by the unusual in life.

What feature or trait do you have that lifts you out of the ordinary? If you were not born with a unique talent, differentiate yourself by developing a positive image. You don't have to be unique to be different. A friend of mine is known as the Gum Man. He carries a pocketful of chewing gum and hands a stick to everyone he meets. Another friend identifies himself by wearing a fresh flower in the lapel of his jacket every day. Silly? Perhaps, but not offensive. And more important, these "labels" became personal trademarks, not overnight but eventually. Reputation is built by repetition.

Visiting the midway at a circus, a carnival, or a county fair gave me a broad, liberal education about the complexities of the human mind. I witnessed in full, living color the words and the unusual aspects of life that motivate people to action. Understanding these foibles and frailties of the human psyche can be valuable knowledge for anyone wanting to perfect their skills in becoming a winner in influencing people.

The barkers, the pitchmen, and pitchwomen, too, were actors who would have won Oscars for their performance had they been on the silver screen. With the introduction of television, these sidewalk pitchmen discovered a new environment for practicing their persuasive skills. Television was virgin territory and these fast-talkers were recruited from carnivals, revival tents and street corners to deliver TV commercials.

To me, being in the company of such persuasive personalities was a free education in human psychology. The fast-talking and the grand promises they made to capture their audience was a dynamic lesson in what not to do. I learned to separate the good from the bad and the lies from the truth. I was imbued with the desire to be able to master the words they used that pierced peoples' mind and compelled them to take action. My desire was to become a master communicator with persuasive sales skills.

In a Senate session in Peloponnesus (Greece) in 400 B.C., during the time of the 400-year war between Athens and Sparta, a senator named Demosthenes challenged a rival senator and orator named Aeskines, saying:

> When you speak, you make them say, 'How well he speaks.'
> But when I speak, I make them say, 'Let's march against Philip.'

Demosthenes, of course, was referring to Philip of Macedon, father of Alexander the Great. As you know from your history studies, Demosthenes was the famous Greek orator who conquered his stuttering impediment by placing small pebbles in his mouth to change his delivery. He became an eloquent orator, a great communicator. He knew that to generate *action* was the prime purpose of any conversation.

I learned another communication and selling lesson from my days of writing classified advertisments. I had written an ad for a pharmaceutical company. The man liked it and asked me to write some mail order copy for him, which I did. I wrote some beautiful prose telling what the product was and the care with which it was made. As he read my copy he shook his head, crumpled the letter and tossed it in the wastebasket, telling me, "Bob, in order to sell this stuff, you've first got to make them need it then make certain they want it badly enough to buy it."

Impressed with this wisdom, I wrote advertising copy that fixed a problem in the reader's mind. The headline was:

DON'T LET FATIGUE POISON YOUR LIFE.

Then I offered his product as a solution. As a clincher, I included a coupon good for ten cents off the purchase price. It worked. I was selling by mail and enjoying it.

This success launched me into writing direct mail sales letters. One customer asked me, "How much do you want for writing a letter." With some apprehension, I said ten dollars. "Highway robbery," he barked back. Then he asked, "How much to correct one I've already written?" Very apologetically, I replied, "Would five dollars be okay?" To which he responded, "Five dollars? Well, okay, but it better be good or I'm not going to pay you anything." Times were tough, it was the mid-1930s and the Depression was in full swing, so I took the offer. I rewrote his entire letter and delivered my masterpiece to him. As he reached for my letter, he said, "Let's see if you know how to write good sales copy." I clutched my golden prose to my chest, reluctant to hand it over to him, saying, "Give me the five dollars first, please!"

Four years later, I graduated from the University of Southern California. On graduation day, I paid off the final installment of my tuition and received my diploma. The average person couldn't see the inscription, but I could. It read: "Paid in Full with wages and commissions earned through the power of sales communication." That same day I exchanged my $250 college wardrobe for a United States Marine Corps uniform. The year was 1941.

Five years later, in 1946, I bought a partnership in a direct mail advertising agency. For me, it was the best of two worlds. I loved the thrill of selling and advertising was salesmanship in print; it was a winning combination.

Then I met Elliott, and he helped sharpen my mind to the power of selling.

4 Using Words to Motivate

Every adversity brings with it the seed of an equivalent success.

—W. Clement Stone

You'll discover Elliott's story to be both fascinating and inspirational. He had a "feel" for saying the right words to communicate his thoughts and his feelings to others. He knew how to use words to motivate and influence others to see things in the proper perspective.

The focus of this book is how to use words to communicate your thoughts and your feelings to others, and you will find that Elliott's story is an effective example.

Elliott was a salesman, but the principles of communication are the same regardless of your profession. If you are a musician, you want to sell your music to a publisher; a math teacher, you are selling students the value of education; a doctor, you are selling patients the value of good health. Learning how to use words to communicate with others will help you change your life for the better.

I met Elliott in 1945. The war was over, and four million service men and women, still with the sound of the bugle blowing reveille, recall and taps ringing loud and clear in their ears, were released into civilian life once again. I was one of them.

All of us were driven by the desire to jump-start our war-delayed careers and to fashion a new life for ourselves. A potpourri of talent descended on the labor market—professionals, professors, construction workers, musicians, bosses, and chiefs—all had dreams of a good life of peace and a well-paying job.

Some were successful; others less so. Why was this? I believe the answer is that some people are much better than others in talking their way into a good job. They have a feel for saying the right words at the right times to get what they want. Learning how to say the right thing at the right time is a talent that can be learned and perfected with practice.

At the end of WWII there was a massive rush for automobiles, home appliances, and consumer goods that had been in short supply during the war. Factories could not keep up with the demand.

Then came the turnaround. Inventories exceeded demand, and products became competitive commodities. It was no longer sufficient to tell people "We've got it" and wait for them to come and get it. Businesses were forced to apply principles of sales and psychology to use the right words to communicate the good news of availability to the consuming public.

I was committed to a career in advertising and selling. When the opportunity came along to purchase an interest in an advertising agency specializing in direct mail, I grabbed it. Direct mail advertising was primarily sales promotion, and this required excellence in both the written and the spoken word. It was just the right combination for me.

I knew I had a lot to learn, and I remembered the sage advice given by one of my college professors. He asked me, "Son, what do you want to do when you graduate?" I quickly replied, "I want to start an advertising agency of my own and make money." To which he interjected, "Oh! Really! You don't intend to be in business very long then, do you?" Then he admonished me, saying, "As a service business, your number one priority is to serve the needs of your customers. Do this and profits will come. But if profit is your main motive, you have no reason for being in a service business."

Starting an advertising agency didn't require much capital, but it did cry for the right people. I had read about Andrew Carnegie and how he had built a colossal industrial empire. He always attempted to find people with brains. He was not referring to people with high IQs, but people possessed with wisdom, curiosity, common sense, and imagination. Carnegie surrounded himself with people who could do the things that he couldn't do. And he wanted people who could *think*.

Carnegie wanted people who could *think* and make ideas come to life. Carnegie Steel was emerging as an industrial force. Carnegie had just installed the Bessemer process for converting brittle iron to flexible steel. In construction everywhere, wood gave way to steel. Bridges, railroads, and ships were waiting to be built—and urgently needed. Carnegie needed people with vision who could bridge the gap between the inception of an idea and its production, and then communicate the benefits to other builders. He needed people with sales skills who could breathe life into these innovative ideas and grab the opportunities as they were presented.

Carnegie's tombstone is engraved with the words:

> Here lays a man who was able to surround himself with men far cleverer than himself.

Then I met a man who fit the criteria set by Carnegie. His name was Elliott. He was a successful salesman, sales manager, speaker, teacher, "coach," and writer. His sales principles and techniques had been field-tested. He possessed all the skills I wanted to learn.

By the end of our first meeting at a business luncheon, I knew I wanted to get to know him. He was in the twilight years of his life, and he wanted to share his passion for selling with whoever would listen. I was there at the right time, and he agreed to take me under his wing and tutor me in the rich rewards of a career in selling. He agreed to come and work with me—not *for* me, but *with* me.

Elliott didn't fit the traditional image of a successful salesman. Your first reaction might be the same as mine: "How could a man scarred and disfigured as he was ever become a successful salesman?

Elliott's story is both remarkable and inspiring. As a young boy, he was filled with big dreams. He was born and raised in a rural town near the Iowa-Illinois border (i.e., the Mississippi). He had dreams of growing up and moving to the big city of Chicago, where he would carve a career for himself in business and make a lot of money. An overturned kerosene lamp started a devastating fire that abruptly changed the direction of his life.

Here is his fascinating story (in my words):

I had just turned fourteen. As a teenager, I was beginning to let my imagination run rampant with visions of pretty girls, dancing, and all the pleasures of being young.

The smell of smoke jarred me wide awake one morning and I discovered that I was trapped in my bedroom. Fearing I was going to die, I crawled through a cloud of smoke and clawed my way through a wall of flame. I lunged through a burning door and collapsed in the front yard. My clothes were on fire and neighbors came to my rescue. In the small rural hospital my blistered hands and face were treated and bandaged.

Several months later, I recovered enough to get my first look at myself in the mirror. It frightened the hell out me. My hands were swollen and stiff, and my face didn't look any better. This predated the use of plastic surgery as burn therapy. Time healed some of the damage to my appearance, but each morning as I peered into the mirror, I was saddened by what I saw. By sheer determination, I healed myself.

"Okay," I responded, "but tell me, Elliott, what made you decide to be a salesman?"

Because of my appearance, I became a recluse. Afraid to expose myself to the stares and what I thought would be the pity of my peers, I hid from view in my upstairs bedroom, watching my friends walking by, wishing I could join them, but too embarrassed to make the move.

From my window I watched the traveling merchants selling their wares from door-to-door. They sold all kinds of merchandise—pots and pans, needles and thread, clothing, and shoes. These direct sellers— hawkers, traders, peddlers, and general itinerant merchants—brought the newest fashions and merchandise to rural America. Some walked door-to-door. Others drove horse-drawn wagons. The more affluent drove Model "T" Fords. All were laden with merchandise to sell to people who were eagerly awaiting their call and to view the latest merchandise from the big city.

If there is such a thing as an epiphany, I had one. I

watched these merchants on their appointed rounds. As they went from door-to-door, I noticed that most were greeted with fond anticipation. Some people invited them into their homes. Others followed them to their wagons to see their wares. Always it was a happy meeting. Few closed the door on these traveling merchants.

Seeing this procession week after week, I had a sudden awakening. It was a revelation that turned my life around. These merchants were meeting people face-to-face. They were greeted warmly. They were not an interruption in people's lives. They were a pleasant interlude, offering new innovations that stirred the imagination and conjured visions of happiness and joy.

Wow, I thought to myself, here I am hiding from my friends, afraid to venture out and expose my scarred hands and face. Watching the sales action before me, I suddenly realized: *People weren't interested in me. They were interested in themselves.*

Right then and there, I changed the attitude that had crippled my outlook for so many years. I vowed I was going to become a salesman and communicate good news to everyone I met. I vowed to 'stop whining and start living.' I prevailed upon my father to help me. He searched and found a man who wanted to sell his business and retire. My dad bought it for me, and I was in business.

My years gazing out the window taught me one invaluable lesson: The very first and most important sale I had to make was *Selling Me on Myself.* I had to convince *me* that I had the power within myself to overcome and obliterate any negative reactions I might have regarding my ability to meet and communicate with people.

It was tough to knock on the first few doors. I wondered how people would react to seeing me. One magic incident eliminated my concerns.

One of my customers, Elsie by name, bought a beautiful blue party dress from me. She wanted to be the belle of the ball at a church social on Sunday. But I didn't have the right color shoes to match her dress. So I drove ten miles to another, larger town, where I found the matching shoes. I paid the regular retail price for them and traveled the ten miles back to present my find.

My heart was pounding in my chest as I knocked on the door. Elsie opened it. Holding up the shoes for her to see, I said 'Elsie, now you're going to be the best-dressed lady at your church social.' With this she pushed open the door and threw her arms around my neck and, kissing each cheek of my scarred face, said, 'Elliott, when you talk to me you make me feel so good.'

At that moment, those eleven words—*when you talk to me you make me feel so good*—revealed to me the secret of salesmanship. People are attracted to people who make them feel good, make them feel important, and make them feel happy. *People may not remember the words you used or the way you looked, but they will remember how you made them feel.*

The secret attraction is that people are connected to people who care about them. Her kisses on my cheek made *me* feel good, too. It was the quid pro quo (literally, 'this for that'). As the Romans say, 'You do something nice for me, and I will return the favor by doing something nice for you.'

Then he asked, "In college, did you study psychology?" I answered "Yes, I had one class in human psychology and what makes people tick." Then Elliott responded, "Top communicators understand psychology and one of the first rules is reciprocity. People feel obligated to repay a kindness. Every sales transaction is an exchange of a benefit from one to another—better expressed as a meeting of minds.

"Think of the customer's mind as a mental teakettle filled with water. The *thought* is the idea you suggest to your customer. This sparks a *feeling* that ignites the desire. When the feeling reaches 212 degrees Fahrenheit, you get steam, which is *action*, and the sale is made. Think of it this way:

A THOUGHT plus a FEELING equals an ACTION.

"This is how the mind works."

Seeing I was riveted by his life story, he continued, "To be a master salesman you must be a master communicator, and this involves a mastery of the English language. Words are the salesman's ammunition. Words are the bullets that travel from one mind to another with lightning speed.

"Great leaders and great salespeople," Elliott continued, " have a mastery of words. Abe Lincoln was a master at telling yarns and stories." As he pulled a piece of paper from his pocket, Elliott said, "I refer to this regularly to remind me that being able to use words is a virtue that overcomes any differences of attire or appearance." Then he proceeded to read this story: A reporter sent to report on Lincoln's Cooper Union address wrote the following that was included as a preface to his report of Lincoln's Cooper Union speech:

> When Lincoln rose to speak, I was greatly disappointed. He was tall, oh so tall, and so angular and awkward that I had for an instant a feeling of pity for so ungainly a man. His clothes were black and ill fitting, badly wrinkled as if they had been jammed carelessly into a small trunk. His bushy head with the stiff black hair thrown back was balanced on a long and lean head-stalk, and when he raised his hands in an opening gesture, I noticed they were very large. He began in a low tone of voice—as if he were used to speaking outdoors and was afraid of speaking too loud.
>
> He said, 'Mr. Cheerman,' instead of 'Mr. Chairman,' and employed many other words with an old-fashioned pronunciation. I said to myself, 'Old fellow, you won't do; it's all very well for the Wild West, but this will never go down in New York.' But pretty soon, he began to get into the subject; he straightened up, made regular and graceful gestures; his face lighted as with an inward fire; the whole man was transfigured.
>
> I forgot the clothing, his personal appearance, and his individual peculiarities. Presently, forgetting myself, I was on my feet with the rest, yelling like a wild Indian, cheering the wonderful man. In the closing parts of his argument you could hear the gentle sizzling of the gas burners.

"You see," Elliott counseled, "the power to move people with words will overcome all other human deficiencies or peculiarities. Top-level sales people are Master Communicators."

Then, with a thoughtful lifting of the eyebrow, said, "Stop to think for a minute: the word *Salesman* has a different connotation. The title of *Salesman* denotes an image of huckster and con man, but it is an honorable and essential function in our economy. The title *Master Communicator* lifts us to a higher level of society."

Looking me in the eye, he offered:

From now on we are going to become *Master Communicators*, but our mission is to sell. Being a salesman is the noblest and the oldest of all professions. You provide people value in their lives. People will spend money only when the value of what they bought is worth more to them than the money with which they part.

As a salesman, you are *a purchase adviser*, helping people make the right decision, showing them the benefits they will enjoy and assuring them they have made the right decision. Too many salespeople look on selling as an adversarial conflict with the challenge being to beat prospects into submission.

Selling is not conflict, argument, or adversarial confrontation. It is a dialogue of meaningful information flowing from one mind to another, with the action being acceptance or rejection. Top-level sales-people thrive on this interaction and winning a sale. To a salesperson, one Yes diminishes a dozen Noes. To be a good salesperson, you must be the supreme optimist and a happy loser when you miss making a sale. 'Winning the sale' means that both parties won.

The most basic human skill is the ability to communicate with each other and to exchange goods and services. In the earliest of times, people exchanged weapons, tools, pottery, and agricultural products. The barter and exchange of goods was the rule of the day.

In the earliest civilizations of Greece, Syria, Egypt, Asia, and the Roman Empire, these early salespeople were referred to as peddlers. Society depended on these peddlers and protected them. They were the contact with the outside world, and they brought all the good things of life to light as they peddled their wares from village to village. They roamed freely in foreign lands, protected by law should any enemy cause them trouble. The laws of the land even assured these 'Peddlers' of adequate compensation.

These peddlers were direct sellers who brought goods from far away places to the local villages. They sold, bought, exchanged, bartered, and catered to the needs and wants of their customers in every conceivable way. Practically every culture in the world shares in the heritage of direct selling. They were the adventurers, the pioneers, and the scouts who braved winding and raging rivers, crossed mountain barriers, and built roads to shrink distance and bring commerce to the world.

More than this, they were the very first diplomats and ambassadors. They were the communicators who brought the cultures of unknown and unexplored lands of the world together in commerce.

Possibly the most famous direct seller-trader was Marco Polo. He was a Venetian trader (a *salesman*) and explorer who gained fame and a place in history for his worldwide travels. He was one of the first Westerners to travel the Silk Road to China. His expeditions brought silk and jade and the riches of the Far East to people who were eager for new innovations and merchandise to tease their taste and please their appetites for new and exotic things.

Give Marco Polo credit also for the development of cartography and cosmology—all of which led to voyages of exploration many years later. All this attributed to an itinerant Salesman who had a driving desire to make his life one of accomplishment.

In the great Mongol Empire, Marco became a friend of the grand Kublai Khan. The Khan took a liking to Marco. He was delighted with Marco's stories and tales of other lands.

Marco was the archetype of the perfect salesman. He was a communicator, a merchant and a 'Peddler' who brought the then known world together through trade and understanding.

Then Elliott capped his soliloquy with,

> "See, College Boy [that's what he called me], a career in sales and advertising can be a challenging and rewarding profession."
>
> Salesmanship is the catalyst that brings good ideas to light and to life. Every success begins with an idea, and every idea springs from men and women who possess a vivid imagination. Even if you don't want a career in sales, you—whoever you are, whatever you do professionally—will need to communicate the value of your abilities and your ideas if you want to accomplish anything.

During my internship with this man, which spanned several years, there was never a dull moment. He was always teaching, and I was absorbing his wisdom. Elliott always corrected me when I would refer to anyone with whom we were doing business as a *client*. He corrected me, saying, "Clients are for lawyers. We're in sales, and they are our *customers*." Then he went on to explain that the word *customer* originated from the Greek word for *custom*—people who make a custom of buying from you again and again; therefore, they are *customers, not clients*." That notion is true regardless of your profession. For example, students are the customers of teachers and patients of doctors. And the better they communicate with each other, the more positive the outcome . . . for both of them.

One of our customers, an appliance wholesaler, sold home appliances through sales representatives and retail stores. The salespeople on whom he depended for sales were a motley crew. Our assignment was to develop a sales training program to lift their level of competence and to train them in the value and benefits of our merchandise.

Because of the geography, size of the territory, and the diversity of sales skills, we elected to publish a monthly journal that was titled *Selling Slants*. Our objective was to move people to become sales communicators. *Selling Slants* featured the "Four I's"—*I*deas that *I*nstruct, *I*nform and *I*nspire.

The targeted sales staff selected for training ran the gamut from order-taker to service salespeople:

- The *order-taker* made a lot of sales calls, but usually didn't know how to ask for the order.

- The *glad-hander* was a charmer who concentrated on selling himself instead of the product. This person mistook sociability for salability.

- The *high-pressure person* was a forceful, aggressive, one-call pitchman, not interested in building up accounts. His only interest was to hit and run—get the one-time commission and disappear.

- The *service salesperson* was good at handling details and rendering service, but lacked initiative. This person was just a "caddy" who helped the customer play the game exactly as the customer wanted.

Our assignment: Take this disparate group of salespeople, men and women, and point them all in the same direction of becoming *Master Sales Creators,* to make them into purchase advisors and business builders, people with imagination, initiative, and resourcefulness who would be welcomed into any office because they always had a sound profit-making idea or valuable information to share. This we called the four 'I's'—Ideas to Instruct, Inform, Inspire.

This was a daunting task. Our challenge was how to inspire these people to action.

Elliott had the answer: "Let's use the narrative persuasive technique." "Okay," I said, "What's that?" Here's how he explained it to me:

There are four types of writing, and these are powerful sales persuaders, too:

1. **Expository writing:** This is newspaper reporting, where you assume people have an interest in reading what you are writing about.

2. **Descriptive writing:** This style is great for selling travel and food. It is filled with adjectives and adverbs.

3. **Persuasive writing:** This is the kind of writing that urges people to take a specific action and gives them a reason why it would be to their advantage to comply with

your reasoning. Verbs encourage movement and generate action.

4. **Narrative writing:** This is storytelling or giving an
account of something.

When you combine narrative with persuasion, you have a
powerful combination for opening the mind and planting new
thoughts that stay and develop and grow. For example, Walt
Disney was a master storyteller whose Mickey Mouse, Donald
Duck, Pluto, and Snow White and the Seven Dwarfs captured
the psyche of people around the world.

As a capper, he asked me, "Didn't your mother, dad, and grandparents
put you to bed each night reading you the Grimm's Brothers stories:
*Jack and the Beanstalk, Cinderella, The Three Little Pigs, Goldilocks and
the Three Bears*, and the like? Fairy tales stimulate the imagination, and
the imagination spawns exciting ideas."

Every month for the next two years we published *Selling Slants*.
Each issue was filled with stories of how average salespeople became
master persuaders. We called on Abe Lincoln, Elias Howe, and Isaac
Singer to reinforce the power of salesmanship.

On Abe Lincoln we wrote:

No man in American history is dearer to the hearts of people
than our sixteenth President, a self-educated lad from the
backwoods of Kentucky who led our nation during the most
critical periods in its history.

Lincoln's writings revealed a shrewd knowledge of human
values. One of the most notable public speeches ever made
was his famous Gettysburg Address—a remarkable, awe-
inspiring work that contains a mere 266 words. But one of his
little known preachments was On Persuading Men:

When the conduct of men is designed to be influenced,
persuasion—kind, unassuming persuasion—should be
adopted. It is an old and true maxim that 'a drop of
honey catches more flies than a gallon of gall.'

So with men. If you would win a man to your
cause, first convince him that you are his sincere friend.

Therein is a drop of honey that catches his heart, which, say what he will, when once gained, you will find but little trouble in convincing his judgment of the justice of your cause, if indeed that cause is a just one.

On the contrary, assume to dictate his judgment, or command his action, he will retreat within himself, close all avenues of his head and heart, and though your cause may be naked truth itself and though you throw it with more than Herculean force and precision, you will no more be able to pierce him than to penetrate the hard shell of a tortoise with a rye straw.

Such is man and so must be understood by those who would lead him. Even to his own best interest.

In these four short paragraphs, Lincoln summed up the very essence of a good salesman—a Master Communicator. He defined it as the ability to influence and convince people and win them to you.

Every issue of *Slants* carried stories of sales strategies that paid off in big dollars. We called out Emerson and debunked his aphorism, "If a man will make a better mousetrap than his neighbor, the world will make a beaten path to his door."

No way! Today, winning salespeople have to beat a path to the *buyer's* door. If you wait for buyers to come to you, you're a loser. This was reinforced with stories about Elias Howe, the man who invented the sewing machine. Howe believed the "Mousetrap" idea. He thought all he had to do was wait for the women to come to him and buy his wonderful labor-saving device. Because of this head-in-the-sand thinking, he died penniless. He had to borrow a decent set of clothes in order to attend his wife's funeral.

Then along came an enterprising man named Singer who sent a virtual army of trained communicators door-to-door to persuade housewives to buy his Singer sewing machine. Because of his dedication to selling, his name became a household word the world over.

Every issue of *Slants* was filled with the sweet smell of success— and how to achieve it.

Did this program work? For the first time this company had a unified and directed sale force and a rudder to keep them on the right track. Salespeople were trained, directed, and motivated, and their success was rewarded.

Elliott had magic about him—wisdom garnered from experience and an insatiable desire to excel. He pointed out to me the weakest link in the marketing cycle of bringing products and services to the ultimate consumer: "High-salaried designers and engineers bring new products to life. Then high-salaried sales and marketing executives design advertising and merchandising to bring eager consumers to the sales counters. Then what happens? The final closing of the sale is entrusted to a low-salaried, untrained sales clerk." Then Elliott closed the conversation by saying, "Maybe we should concentrate on training sales clerks and making them high-salaried salespeople."

Now let me introduce you to Frank.

5 How to Listen

A good listener is not only popular everywhere,
but after a while he gets to know something.

—William Mizner

Frank was a master communicator. He earned the respect of everyone he met because he knew how to listen to them. Frank understood human nature and he understood people. His sage counsel to me was, "Asking the right questions gives you the power to take the conversation anywhere you want it to go."

He went on to advise me that if I wanted to be a successful communicator and to win friends that I should learn to ask questions and then master the art of listening.

Frank was nudging eighty-five years of age when I bought his mail order office supply business. I wanted to add a mail order section to my agency. And I wanted Frank's canny savvy and wisdom.

Frank agreed that he would sell me his office supply business and help me with the transition of management until I was able to get it on a paying basis. Then he added one condition, "But you must allow me six weeks leave twice a year." I laughingly agreed when he explained that the time off was to visit his 102-year-old mother who lived in the Midwest.

Frank explained that these visits were tenuous times for him. Mother still insisted on calling him "Sonny" even though he was in his eighties. She was constantly scolding him, saying, "Sonny, you're smoking too much. You don't eat right. You're getting too fat. You're working too hard."

When he returned from one of these visits to mother, Frank told me that his mother's mind was still sharp, but that he worried about her eyesight. "She still sees me as a young man of thirty or forty.

These vacations made him nostalgic about his youth in Missouri. He told me, "As a young kid living in the Bible Belt states, I had very few lifetime work choices. You could become a farmer, go to work for the railroad, work a riverboat, or, if you were so inclined, you could become a preacher." None of these appealed to him, but he knew one thing for certain, that he wanted to earn money. Money, according to Frank, was the key that would open all the treasures and pleasures of life.

Frank had only an eighth-grade education and no family inheritance. The family was broke and lived from day to day. This meant that for him to become a doctor, lawyer, or banker was out of the question.

Uncertain as to what to do with his life, Frank reasoned that he liked being with people, he enjoyed talking and bandying words around, he liked to read books about successful people and he was curious. To this he added that his mother always scolded him for asking too many questions: "She would say to me, 'Son, why do you ask **why** all the time?' I remember that my smart answer got me a slap across the side of my head when I replied, **'Why** shouldn't I ask **Why?'"**

As a young schoolboy, Frank's fondest memories were of congenial impromptu gatherings where he would shoot the bull in unreserved and sometimes intimate conversation. He said that he enjoyed the give-and-take discourse. Frank was very candid when he told me, "We covered every subject, from racy magazines to flirting with girls to philosophic discourse about Prohibition and the state of the union. I loved to talk, but, most importantly, I loved to listen. I always figured I learned more when I listened. I soon discovered the one magic phrase—'Very Interesting, Tell Me More'—that kept the other guys chattering and me learning.

"Soon it became a challenge for me to see how long I could keep someone else talking and spilling their secrets to me without me chiming in. Asking questions and then listening can make you a 'brilliant conversationalist.' Over the years I have perfected four basic questions that will keep a conversation moving without uttering a word:

1. **Ask an Objective, Open-Ended Question** that cannot be answered yes or no. Don't ask, 'Do you think it will rain today?' If the answer is no, the ball is back in your court again. Ask instead, 'What do you think the weather will be like today?' It's impossible to answer yes or no. The answer demands words to express the answer. 'I think it will rain today' or 'I don't think it will rain today.'

2. **Ask a Reflective Question** to follow up on the answer to the original question: 'Oh, where did you get the idea it was going to rain today?' The answer must be expressed verbally: 'I read it in the newspaper.' Then ask a reflective question again, 'What newspaper do you read?'

3. **Ask a Directive Question**. This question keeps you in control of the conversation. If the speaker goes off on a tangent, bring the conversation back on the track you want. Interrupt long enough to ask, 'You mentioned the newspaper you read, the *Daily Star*. What sections do you read?'

4. **Silence.** This is a tough one to handle. It requires finesse and skill. Use it carefully. If there is a lull in the conversation, be mute. Silence. Don't say a word. It is a sure bet the other person will stammer and stutter and break the silence with more conversation. Then you are once again in control."

At this point, I used one of Frank's strategies for listening. I said, "Frank, you're fascinating, tell me more."

Here's the rest of his story, Frank's first job was selling pianos. He didn't have a retail store or any inventory. He represented a major piano manufacturer and sold pianos to churches and schools. This was a very limited market whose replacement factor was practically nil. Pianos lasted a lifetime. All they needed was a tuning now and then. Here he learned a vital lesson in selling: You have to show in a dramatic and memorable way what the product will do and the benefits to be enjoyed.

Fortunately, the times were kind to him, and the piano market picked up. WWI was over; Prohibition was in and was being enforced. Speakeasies, nightclubs and roadhouses sprang up to accommodate the "gotta-have-a-drink" public—all against the law, but thriving.

This was the beginning of the jazz age and new dance crazes. The Charleston was the popular dance and musical tunes ran the extremes from *Yes We Have No Bananas* to *It's Three O'clock in The Morning and We've Danced the Whole Night Through*. Dancing called for music and music needed pianos.

The big boost for Frank was that the public was beginning to want pianos in their homes, so he began selling pianos door-to-door. It was a little tough to sell without the physical instrument to demonstrate. There was no way a piano could be carried door-to-door, so he carried a catalog and photographs of the entire line of pianos from concert grand pianos to inexpensive uprights,

The first sales mistake Frank made turned out to be his best lesson in sales. He thought showing the lowest-priced, low-end models first and then showing the more expensive models would be the better way to sell. He was wrong. Only a few people bought better grade pianos after comparing them to the lower-priced instruments.

Then he switched his presentation and used a touch of psychology. He started by showing the best and highest-priced pianos first, regardless of what the buyer wanted. With this tactic the customer would shop the entire line from the best and most expensive model to the lowest priced model. When people were given an opportunity to select the models from top-down, rather than from bottom-up, the average order was substantially increased—buyers wanted the best, but settled for the in-between model. Frank also carried a portable wind-up Victrola, a record playing machine of the era. It was a modern miracle of the day. All you had to do was wind it up, put on a record, put the phonograph needle in place, flip the play switch, and suddenly beautiful music would fill the room—everything from Beethoven to the jazzy Charleston. It was a bit heavy to lug around, but it worked. The piano company also had a self-teaching instruction book that took piano lovers by the hand and showed them how to play the seven basic musical notes on the eighty-eight keys.

Frank said, "In 1925, my sale of pianos got a boost from a mail order advertisement placed by the U.S. School of Music. They ran an advertisement in magazines with the headline, 'They Laughed When I Sat Down At The Piano. But when I started to play . . . ' The copywriting was a classic; written by John Caples, it was pure salesmanship in print. It made people want to own a piano and learn to play it. The advertisement depicted a real life story of how a man became a social success because he learned to play the piano.

"The advertisement set the emotional scene and read something like this:

'Can he really play?' one girl whispered. 'Heavens no!' Arthur exclaimed. 'He never played a note in his life.' Then, to the amazement of all my friends, I strode confidently over to the piano and sat down. 'Jack is up to his old tricks,' somebody chuckled. The crowd laughed, they were all certain that I couldn't play a single note. Finally I started to play. Instantly a tense silence fell on the guests. The laughter died on their lips as if by magic. I played through the first bars of Beethoven's immortal Moonlight Sonata. I heard gasps of amazement. My friends sat breathless—spellbound . . . '

"This advertisement capped my career as a piano salesman. I obtained a copy of the ad and used it as a sales tool to help me sell pianos.

"Every time I made a sale, I would ask for the name of the neighbor or friend who might share the same love of music. I always received the names of one or two good prospects. When I knocked on the recommended friend's door and it was opened, I would say, 'Good morning, Mrs. Williams. Your good friend, Mrs. Smith, told me that you two share a love for music. What is your favorite musical instrument?' This personal touch made me more than an ordinary door-to-door salesman. I was a friend calling on the recommendation of a friend.

"Then the sale of pianos dropped. People loved the piano and the music, but they did not want to take the time to learn how to play. Good fortune stepped in again. A new piano was available. It was called a player piano. All you had to do was insert a perforated music roll into the instrument, pump the pedals with your feet and 'presto,' beautiful music. You could watch the piano keys falling and rising as the music played. No lessons required, just sheer enjoyment without the pain of practice."

Frank was dedicated to a life in sales. He was an opportunist, too. He told me that when piano sales became routine he found new sales challenges selling Fuller brushes, Hoover vacuum cleaners, Bissell carpet sweepers and automobiles door-to-door.

Automobiles? This piqued my curiosity, and I asked Frank how in the world he sold cars door-to-door? He explained that his best days were weekends. He would drive his demonstrator around the neighborhoods and anytime he saw a man or woman washing their car he would stop and chat with them. He was quick to add that this was many years before car wash businesses were popular.

His sales theory was that anyone who cared enough to keep their old car polished, clean and shiny was a good prospect for a brand-new polished and shiny car.

Frank told me how he got people interested in buying a new car. He had a mischievous twinkle in his eye (just like the little boy who had discovered a way to hot-wire the family cat) when he explained that he, would get them talking about their favorite cars by asking a question that cannot be answered yes or no. He asked what they liked about their car, followed by a few *what else* and *why* questions to hitchhike on their answers. Soon he knew what stimulated their imagination about a new car. This is the first step to making a sale.

Frank believed that to be a successful salesperson, you must understand that everyone to whom you speak has his or her own unique desires. To be a winner, it is your responsibility to understand the needs, wants, expectations and perceptions of each individual. Only by asking the right questions and then listening with your eyes as well as your ears will you discover the inner feelings and desires of each person you are talking to.

I asked Frank to share with me his secrets for being a successful sales communicator. "No secrets," Frank offered, "just good common sense. I recognize everyone I meet as a special individual. I keep a list of vital information on every contact I make. Regardless of whether or not a sale was made, I follow up with a 'Thank You for the courtesy of talking to me' card—always sent the same day.

"Also, knowing the age of the prospect's car, I would send a greeting card each year on the car's 'birthday.' I would always make an effort to get the birthdays, anniversary, and any other special-event information from every contact. I sent a greeting or congratulation card to recognize these special events. They were just cordial contacts, no sales messages.

"When warranted, if a service or a safety message was timely, the mailings would contain helpful information or suggestions: *Check the wear on your tires for the safety of your family; Fan and timing belts need checking at so many miles to prevent untimely breakdowns, etc. . . .*

"Every contact was designed to inform, instruct and inspire with a new idea or two. Eventually some of these people would call me when they wanted a new car. Better yet, they would recommend friends. I never spent time in a showroom waiting for people to come to me; I went out to the people, door-to-door."

Whenever he sold a car, Frank would canvas the neighborhood close to his buyer's house. He told me, "Bob, people don't want to just keep up with their neighbors, they want to upstage them. In this case, they wanted to buy a car as good as, or preferably better than, the one their neighbor bought."

When he sold a car, Frank built a lifetime relationship. He made a call or sent a card reminding his customers when service was due. He resolved every service problem—personally. Frank earned a customer for life. Frank loved people, and people loved Frank.

I asked him how he maintained all this information and he said that he kept meticulous files on 3" x 5" index cards with dates and times of mailings. It took a lot of time, but paid off handsomely in sales and in personal relations. It's easier to do this same thing today on a laptop. Start today. It will pay you handsome dividends. Never forget: an individual's innermost desire is to be recognized as an individual.

Then I asked, "Tell me, Frank, what was the most interesting or exciting sale you ever made?" Without hesitation he gave me the answer, "By accident." He said, "I happened to be in the distributor's showroom checking on a delivery date for a car I had sold. While waiting, I noticed what looked like a dirt farmer walking into the showroom. He was wearing blue denim bib-front overalls, a plaid flannel shirt, high-laced boots scuffed on the toes, and a straw hat cocked to one side of this head. He had a shadow of a beard. Wire-rimmed glasses punctuated the eyes on his weathered face. At first glance one might have appraised him as a farm worker in town for a haircut, a shave, and a bath at the local barber shop."

"A bath in a barber shop?" I asked. "Sure," Frank answered. "Way back in 1925 in the isolated farm communities, inside plumbing, running water and electricity were highly unusual. Barbershops offered baths as well as shaves and haircuts. Saturdays were come-to-town shopping and personal preening days.

"The red, white, and blue spinning barber poll guided the unshaven and unclean to the appointed place. Barbershops did a thriving business all day long into the late evening hours. As fast as the tubs could be emptied and the water heated, a steady flow of farmers made their entrances and exits from the single tub in the only barbershop in town. Saturdays were reserved for cleanliness, Sundays for Godliness.

"When this 'farmer' walked into the building he sauntered over to a brand spanking new four-door sedan. It was black, the only choice of the day, and it shined to mirror brightness. With its lacquered, wooden-spoke wheels and spare tire mounted in the fender wells, this automobile caught the farmer's eye.

"The lone salesman on the floor, after a single glance at the prospect, turned to me and said, 'Hey, I'm out for a cup of coffee. Get rid of him for me, will you, please.' Then pointing to the farmer with a nod of his head, he whispered to me, 'There ain't no way that farmer can afford that car.' Then he walked out for his coffee.

"As he departed, I walked over to the gentleman. He might have been a 'farmer,' but to me he was at least a prospect on whom I could practice my sales talk. I introduced myself with, 'Hi, my name is Frank'. I didn't wait for him to share his name; I just continued. Giving the car an affectionate touch, I said, 'A beauty, isn't she? Any man would be proud to own this car.'

'Sure is,' the farmer replied. Then he bowled me over when he said, 'I'll take it.'

"I thought to myself, he can't do that. I haven't sold him yet. 'I like that car. I'll take it,' he repeated. He bought the car. The sale was finished. Time for me to shut up and negotiate the terms. Looking at me, he directed me to meet him at the Citizens Bank, Monday morning at 9:00 A.M., and he would give me cash for the car and take delivery.

"I wanted to ask him one more vital question that might just cost me the sale. The question I longed to ask was, 'Can you really afford to buy this car?' But I kept my mouth shut, which was the best judgment call I ever made. He signed the contract and departed. As he walked out of the door, he was pointed in the direction of the barbershop. My parting thought was: Will he be at the bank when it opens on Monday?

"At the appointed hour on Monday morning, the farmer showed up. He was a different man: His hair was trimmed, he was clean-shaven, and I detected a faint fragrance of lilac after-shave lotion. A

$1200 sale without opening my mouth, just as a result of asking one pointless question, 'A beauty, ain't she? Any man would be proud to own this car.'"

I shook my head in disbelief and confirmed to Frank, "That's a fantastic story. It just goes to show that you can't judge a book by its cover." To which Frank added, "And you can't judge a prospect by outward appearance. You'll be wrong every time." Then he said, "I'll give you another thought about people. Do you know why so many people are dissatisfied with what they buy?"

"No, tell me," I responded. Here's what he told me: "You lose customers and friends for many reasons. They die and fade from view, or they become dissatisfied and leave for new associations. It's part of life. You can't avoid it. But the major reason you lose customers and friends too is because of dissatisfaction caused by indifference—as communicators we spend too little time on building better relationships with friends and customers.

This was Frank's life before I had the pleasure of meeting him, but I was curious why a successful communicator would want to start a small mail order office supply business. Why not just retire and enjoy life?

Frank responded by telling me that he enjoyed working. Every day was a new adventure, a new challenge. "I feel useless when I'm not working and meeting people. I enjoy meeting and helping people, making new friends and in so doing to improve my own life." Then Frank added a bit of his own philosophy, telling me, "You know, Bob, you cannot improve your own life when you have no other model but yourself to copy. You only gain wisdom when you listen to other people."

Frank told me that he did try retirement for one day, but that dream came to an abrupt halt on the very first morning of retirement. Here's his account:

"At precisely 7:00 A.M., I woke up to the ringing of the alarm. Realizing I was free from any responsibility, I shut off the alarm and rolled over to enjoy a few more 'Z's.' At that same time my wife nudged me, saying, 'Frank, I have a DAR meeting today. When you get up, would you please tidy up the house, and, if you have time, please take the packages on my desk to the post office. Oh, yes, call the Pawley's and ask Natalie what time they will pick us up this evening.'

"Retirement? I thought to myself, if this is what retirement is, it isn't for me. After doing my 'wifely' chores, I called my lawyer and told him, 'Spence, I've got to go back to work. I've always been interested in a small mail order business. Something I can do without too much hands-on involvement. Do you have any ideas?'"

"Spence scolded me, saying, 'Frank, you just retired; give it a chance.' When I related my shattering experiences of the morning, he promised to help me find a small mail order venture just to keep me out of the house and out of harm's way.

"Several weeks later Spence called me with a great opportunity. 'It's a very small mail order office supply business. You can buy it for the value of the inventory, which is small. Running it will keep you occupied and out of the house and out of doing housework. With your sales and marketing savvy, it will be challenge for you and fun for you to develop it into something.'"

Frank described how he bought the business and developed it into a profitable enterprise. He had a twinkle in his eye when he told me, "Mail order selling was fun and darned exciting. Every day I was called on to make every dollar I spent return a profit. I put into mail order practice every principle of salesmanship, psychology and marketing I had ever learned."

One lesson he learned really paid off. Remembering the customer records he kept when he was selling cars, he applied the same process to selling office supplies. He maintained a record of all purchases customers made. He noticed that one customer ordered five reams of paper every month and had done so on a regular basis. He had an idea that would benefit the customer and save him time and money, too. Frank offered to automatically ship five reams of paper to the customer each month and give him a ten percent discount. The customer would never be inconvenienced by running out of paper and would save money. Frank benefited two ways: He had a guaranteed sale every month and, more important, the customer wouldn't stray to a competitor.

Frank's office products company had nothing to distinguish it from a vast array of competitors in the community. Competitors ranged from small Mom 'n Pop office supply stores to national chains. Frank shopped these stores to determine how his store could be uniquely different. All the competitors were merchandising on lower prices.

According to Frank, "Trying to compete on price alone was like getting into a 'piddling' contest with a bunch of skunks. Plus, price merchandising invites customers to shop the competition for a still lower price." Frank wasn't prepared for this assault, so he positioned his office supply company to be uniquely different.

Frank told me that he did not believe price was a prime motivator. He was certain service and relationship marketing would set him apart from competitors. To do this, he concentrated on the small business market and organized to serve it with the same importance as if it was Bank of America. Delivery, attention to details, and service were the benefits he offered.

As a capper, with every order, large or small, he added something extra. He searched the market for unusual, inexpensive gadgets—a marking pen, a letter opener, or some other unusual office tool—and shared them with his customers. He became known as "the Gadget Guy." It not only made the business different, it made it profitable. And, most important, he had a tremendous amount of *fun* doing it.

Then Frank added a bit of sage advice: "You'll never work a day in your life if you enjoy and have fun doing what you do. Selling is an exciting and stimulating career." Frank continued. "Every day stretches your imagination thinking of ways and words to make you a winner in dealing with people.

"Selling in print is exactly the same as face-to-face selling. Only in print you have to be right the first time. There is no second chance for rebuttal or rephrasing, as there is in face-to-face selling. In mail order you have to say what you mean and mean what you say. You never have a second chance to make a first impression."

It was my lucky day when Frank and I became friends. He was a master communicator in both the spoken and printed word. He was a marketer, a merchandiser, a sales promoter, and salesman all rolled into one.

I learned more about marketing from Frank in just a few months than I did studying four years in college. Here is some sage advice I learned from this old master:

"Too many salespeople allow the immediate and urgent need for commissions to drive out the permanent and important need to build solid customer relationships and friendships, too. Don't let your emotions or immediate needs cloud your good judgment. Build for your future.

"'Marketing' is a bandied-about word that few people can define.

Tell the average person you are in marketing, and they respond to you with, 'Oh, you have a grocery store or a meat market?'

"Marketing begins with the imagination that conceives an idea for the creation of a new product that will solve a well-recognized need in the market place. A good example is the invention of the washing machine. This liberated women from the washboard and copper wash-tubs. The vacuum cleaner relieved women from the hard labor of hanging rugs and carpets over the clothesline and beating the dust out using a wire carpet swatter. Inside plumbing is another classic example. Some years ago, we went to the bathroom outside and ate our meals inside; now we eat outside and enjoy bathroom facilities inside. Times have changed for the better.

"Fuller brushes is another good example of visionary marketing. Founded in 1906 as a door to-door sales organization, Fuller has grown and expanded into a international sales organization with over 2000 products that clean, polish and protect homes and businesses,

"The Fuller Company used good marketing and merchandising to sell their brushes. Salespeople went door-to-door, not selling, but giving. They would hand the lady of the house a free sample brush, inviting her to use it for a week on household chores. The product was good. It sold itself. Allowing sufficient time for testing, the salesperson would return to ask for an order. This provided the opportunity to sell extra products like different brushes for different household situations. Marketing people today call these *line extensions*, but it's common sense: When you can increase the size of an order, you increase the dollar value to you and to your company.

Fuller today, a century after its founding, still uses these same sales principles—a free gift with every purchase. But, technology has changed the way they do business. Door-to-door with a free gift is still Fuller's sales strategy but a web site and the Internet is the medium they use to expand their reach internationally. As in every organization, sales and marketing principles remain constant, but modern day technology shrinks distance and makes the world the market.

"Here's where psychology becomes a closely associated ally to clinching the sale. The psychological principle applied to the sale of Fuller brushes is called *reciprocity*. Whenever you give someone a gift that has a perceived value, there is an innate driven desire that kicks in and says, 'I should return the favor.' In our daily lives we feel it is essential to return favors.

"When someone gives you a gift, your emotion tells you to reciprocate and return a gift of equal or perceived value. Did you ever receive a Christmas gift from someone who is not on your list? When this happens, you usually scurry around to find a gift of equal value so you can reciprocate the thoughtfulness.

"It is a very human emotion to feel obligated to return a favor. I used this human reaction to my advantage in selling. When I sold a well-branded product that lent itself to sampling, I would offer a 30-day or 90-day free trial period to prove the product's value. Generally this would result in a sale. The only caveat was that the product had to be as good as you said it was. I had to be realistic in making product promises. I was truthful and didn't use sales and advertising 'puffery' to promise more than the product could deliver.

"Master Communicators have a command of the principles of psychology, sociology, and anthropology. Anyone who wants the power to persuade and favorably influence others needs to have command of these principles. Psychology deals with the human mind's mental and emotional behavior. Sociology deals with the science of human interrelationships, and anthropology is concerned with customs and social relationships.

"Master these principles, and you will be in command whenever you are trying to persuade or motivate a person to your way of thinking. Notice I said *motivate*, not manipulate—there is a difference. To motivate is to urge someone to do something because it is good for them and to their benefit, reinforced with a lot of Reasons Why. To manipulate is to influence in an unfair and fraudulent way. Master Communicators motivate."

Picking Franks brain one afternoon, I asked him a question (just as he taught me to do): "What are the other psychological forces that a Master Communicator should know and practice?"

He responded, "Everyone has a Hot Button that sparks the flame and ignites the desire to act or do something. I certainly am not a psychologist, but I can share with you a few things I have learned about the hot buttons that jolt people to action. Here are a few principles of psychology that will impact your ability to move people in your direction and to your way of thinking. First and foremost is *self-interest.*

People are interested in themselves. They want to know how they can enjoy the good things in life and eliminate things that cause them pain and suffering: 'What's in it for me?' (WIIFM) is the paramount question in everyone's mind. In tandem with this add MMFG(I), 'Make me feel good' (or important).

"People may not remember what you said to them, but they definitely will remember how you made them feel. This is especially true in charitable giving. Often too much emphasis is given to the good your contribution will do for others instead of how good you will feel for having given to help others. Some sage summed this up when he said, 'There is no greater calling than to serve your fellow man, and there is no greater *satisfaction* than to have done it well.' The key word is *satisfaction*: How good it will make me feel for having done it well.

"Next is *liking*. People respond favorably to you for two reasons: number one, they like you and number two, they like what you are saying or selling.

"When someone you like or respect asks you to do something and you feel that person has your best interests in mind, you have a good feeling that you should honor his request: *People like to say 'Yes' to people they like.*

"As human beings, we have a tendency to like and favor people who are similar to us. We lean towards people who have similar likes, dislikes, strengths, or frailties. I don't like men who can grow manly beards. The reason for my dislike? I can't grow a full beard. And, I don't like people who smoke. I quit smoking last year and I resent people who still smoke.

"When selling, I never dress flamboyantly. No excess jewelry or lotions. I wear conservative clothing—no excesses or extravagances. I do nothing to call attention to myself. I only want to call attention to my product and the solution it delivers. My focus is to make my customer feel good about doing business with me and about the solution my product offers." Frank quickly qualified this remark with, "This is my persona; this is the personal image I want to project to others. Everyone is a unique individual, so project the image of yourself with which you are comfortable. Be yourself!

"Next is *social acceptance*. Individuals generally want to conform to the accepted standards of society. Many times the acceptance of an idea, a product or a service hinges on what other people think about it.

Uncertainty is a deterrent to making up one's mind. People do not want to make mistakes. To avoid the embarrassment of making a wrong decision, people turn to recognized authorities, experts, or trusted friends to help them decide.

"I went shopping with my wife and daughter. My wife was trying to choose between two dresses. Uncertain and not wanting to make a foolish mistake, she turns to my daughter and asks, 'Which one looks the best on me?' She is looking for social approval. She knows which one she likes best, but she wants her buying decision reinforced. *Four questions* need to be answered to encourage people to make a decision:

1. What will this product do for me?
2. What does this product say about me?
3. How will it impress my friends or associates?
4. How will this product make me feel about myself?

"Every day we are influenced by what other people demonstrate as being correct. Bartenders 'seed' the tip jar, not with coins, but with folding paper money. This says to the customer, 'It is customary for people to leave a tip, paper money—not loose change. Other people do it, so should you.' Go to a restaurant. When the bill comes, it often suggests how much the gratuity should be—15 percent, 18 percent or 20 percent. People want to conform.

"Buyers rely on the statements of others to help them make up their minds. Use of case histories is another way to reinforce the decision-making process. McDonald's, in its introductory years, demonstrated the acceptance of its hamburgers. At key locations there was an eye-stopping, animated sign that recorded every hamburger ordered by customers in the entire McDonald's chain. The sign clicked off the number of hamburgers served the second they were sold. The sign clicked-off figures in the billions second-by-second. This demonstration gave social proof the burgers certainly must be good—billions of people were buying and eating them at all times of the day.

"Let's take a look at the power of *authority* in moving people to action. Think about it! You're speeding down the highway and in your rear-view mirror you spot a police cruiser. Your immediate reaction is to slow down because you know that patrolman has the power to give you a ticket for speeding. Your physician suggests you stop smoking—

or else! You listen because there is power in his medical authority. Your automobile is starting to hiccup and cough; you go to a mechanic and he tells you a major overhaul is needed. You're not a mechanic, but he is, and he has the power and authority of mechanical knowledge to persuade you to place your car in his capable hands.

"We tend to like products, services or ideas that are endorsed by recognized experts or authorities or people we know—particularly if they are someone we like or respect. It is always a good idea to lace your conversation liberally with case histories and testimonials of authorities and others who have bought, used, or tested your product. Perceived authorities are powerful motivators. Any person who possesses the skills you do not and to whom you turn in times of need has the *power of authority* in your mind.

"Take your own situation," Frank suggested. "You want to become a top-level salesman and a communicator in both the spoken and printed word. Then set your goal to *earn* the respect of all with whom you come in contact. Notice I said *earn*. Strive to be perceived as an authority in all that you do. Learn your communication skills and know the products you sell so well that you have the power to be respected as a *purchase advisor*. You can call this *commitment* and *consistency*.

"Now if you want to increase the value of something, use the psychological principle of *scarcity*. People assign more value to things when they are perceived to be limited in the number produced or limited in the quantity available. When you go to a store and you see a sign that says, 'Limited Supply, only one to a customer,' the little value scale in your head tells you to buy and you snap up your reserved 'Only One to a Customer'. But when the sign advises 'Only Two to a Customer,' your immediate impulse is to double your value and you grab not one, but two. This adds up to double the dollar sales for the merchant. People are motivated to act when scarcity is perceived.

"Remember when I told you how I sold pianos? I told you that I always introduced the best and highest priced piano first. This principle in sales is called *perceptual contrast*. When two items are different from each other, put them together to demonstrate the difference. Always introduce the top-of-the-line first, then fall back to the financial comfort level of the customer.

"This applies to any product regardless of price—automobiles, real estate, and other luxury items. Perceptual contrast generally gives people a logical reason to buy the product that will deliver superior value and personal satisfaction than the lesser-priced product they originally intended to buy.

"Isn't that manipulating people? I asked.

"Absolutely not," Frank responded. "People buy products to satisfy a need or want. As a sales advisor, you are guiding them to buy the product that will deliver the highest satisfaction and value.

"Selling is not talking someone into buying something they don't want. People like to buy, they like to shop. The job of the salesperson is to make it easy for people to make the right and most satisfying decision. Remember, too, people cannot be manipulated or compelled to buy something they do not want. People buy because they want to.

"As a sales counselor and advisor, it is your job to help people make up their minds. You do this by giving them *Reasons Why* it would be in their best interest to buy the product from you, not from competitors. Giving people logical *reasons why* they should buy is more powerful than relying on persuasive tactics.

"When I was selling automobiles, I used *reasons why* liberally and generously to convince my customer that buying the car from me was making a wise decision. I relied on five prime *reasons why*, each of which gave my customer a logical benefit for buying:

1. **Transportation** (a basic benefit). This is an automobile; it has four wheels, an engine, and a steering wheel. You should buy this car because it is good transportation. It will get you from where you are to where you want to be faster than walking.

2. **Speed and Comfort** (added benefits). This car has innovative new amenities and is equipped with air ride suspension. This car will not only get you there faster, but also in luxurious comfort.

3. **Price and Value** (practical benefits). The low price and the public acceptance of this car is why the model will retain its value for you.

4. **Safety** (expanded benefit). This sparks an emotion about the safety and protection for your family. The reinforced frame and impact bumpers will protect you and your family and are other reasons why you should own this car.

5. **Pride and Ego** (emotion and fantasy). You'll be the pride of

your neighborhood. Your friends will envy you, and you will feel a flush of satisfaction for having made this wise decision. Emotion and fantasy can be more powerful persuaders than product benefits. People buy things they want to the detriment of things they need.

"The principles of humanistic psychology were developed by Abraham Maslow. He held that there are five levels of human need. As each level is satisfied, humans move to the next higher level of attainment, or under adverse conditions, they fall back to the lower level. The five needs are:

1. **Physical**—the need for food, clothing and shelter to endure the environment.

2. **Survival**—the need for the right food, protective clothing and shelter to prevail over life.

3. **Social**—the need for association with others, to interact and be accepted.

4. **Ego**—the need for personal recognition, motivated by the emotions and the senses. An individual views everything in relation to himself. In communications, touching the right sense is a powerful persuader. Emotion is the nerve center of the body.

5. **Self-Attainment**—the desire and the drive to be an achiever, to be liked, to be a winner in dealing with others. This is where fantasy takes over.

"There," Frank said, "you have the story of my business life." Then he added, "You are now the proud owner of your very own mail order office supply business. Sharing my skills and experience with you is my way of paying back all the good luck and success I have enjoyed the last eighty plus years."

With Frank's sales and marketing skills, I developed the business into a profitable enterprise. Several years later, I sold the business to a major office supply company.

6 How You Can Be a Winner

The ability to deal with people is as purchasable a commodity as sugar or coffee. And I will pay more for that ability than for any other under the sun.

—John D. Rockefeller

People are still at the heart of everything we do. And the ability to deal favorably and amicably with people is a priceless commodity. Both John D. Rockefeller and Andrew Carnegie valued this ability above all others. The power to persuade is an important talent, but the ability to communicate intelligently to win people to your cause is essential to your success. Technology can be wonderful, but "people skills" still come first. Leadership demands that you be a winner in dealing with people. There is a way to set your internal compass to guide you through life and make you a winner in dealing with people

Leadership in the art of communication is more about what you can cause other people to do and less about what you do yourself. Every leader in history, ancient, past and present, possessed the power to communicate, which was the force that won people to their cause.

A long time ago I learned that all behavior is caused. Every human response is the result of words or actions that trigger a reaction, whether favorable or combative. The other day I noticed a young boy sporting a multihued black eye. It looked like Aladdin's magic lamp. Curious about how he came by the shiner, I asked him, "Son, who gave you the black eye?" His brilliant answer was, "Mister nobody *gave* it to me, I had to *fight* for it." You see, all behavior, good or bad, is caused.

Every day the news on television and in newspapers reports: Inability to communicate causes social unrest. Parents cannot communicate with their children. Teachers cannot communicate with students. Businesspeople cannot communicate with employees and customers. Diplomats mired in conflict. United Nations at impasse.

If by some chance:

- You are the proud parent of well-disciplined and intelligent children,
- Your marriage is all peaches and cream,
- You have many friends and favorably influence all with whom you come into contact,
- You are eminently satisfied with your lot in life and all your dreams have come true.

If this is you, then skip to the next chapter.

If not, read on.

If you want to begin building your skills as a communicator and a leader, you will find undiscovered personal value by going off the beaten track. Begin by practicing to be a winner in your everyday contacts—with your wife or husband, children, friends, associates, strangers you meet. For most people, 80 percent of their waking hours are spent communicating with other people. This offers you all kinds of opportunities to develop your skills as a communicator.

Here are some proven tactics you can use to hone and sharpen your skills. Practice these principles in every personal contact, and you will perfect and strengthen your communication skills and become a winner in dealing with people. Remember, all conversation involves *selling skills*—you are selling an idea, thought, proposition, product, service or yourself as a brilliant conversationalist.

Here are twelve cardinal principles of conversation and selling that master communicators use to win the respect, trust, confidence or compliance of people. Practice these principles during every daily contact you make. Do this and you will discover the magic of *How to talk so people will listen to you and how to listen so people will talk to you.*

Cardinal Principle 1

Perception

You are not in control of any conversation until you *understand* the other person's point of view. *Understand* is the key word. Your first and foremost position in any conversation is to understand the other person's point of view. There can be no communication until there is a meeting of minds, a common understanding of each other's point of view. Until the conversation is put into the proper perspective, the discourse will devolve into argumentative conflict or quarreling. Neither one wins, both lose.

When two people see or experience the same set of circumstances, seldom do they interpret them in exactly the same way. Each has a different perspective, and each behaves as if their perspective is the correct one. With this difference of opinion it is practically impossible to communicate effectively with one another.

The only way on earth to influence the other fellow is to talk about what he wants and show him how to get it. This was the sage advice of Dale Carnegie in his book *How to Win Friends and Influence People*. The key is to find out what the person wants. Knowing what really matters to him can help you to persuade him to do what you want him to do.

There are several techniques for establishing the common ground. One way is to use the direct approach: Ask a direct (or "directive") question:

> "John, what's bugging you?"
> "Mac, I can see something is bothering you. What's the problem?"
> "Tell me, Joe, where do you hurt?"

There is no way I can relieve Joe's pain until I know the exact spot where Joe hurts.

When you are concerned that the person you are talking to may resist or resent the direct approach, use the indirect approach:

> "John, I'm trying to find out more about this matter. What is your opinion?"

Or, you might try the weasel tactic:

> "Joe, I don't know much about this subject. What is your opinion?"

Using the objective question technique (a question that cannot be answered yes or no), you align the conversation on a firm foundation of mutual understanding. From this point on you can be in control by asking questions that reflect on the answer that was given.

When you asked for Joe's opinion and he replies, "I was convinced by an article in the *Economist* magazine," you keep Joe talking by reflecting on his answer, saying, "Joe, that's fascinating. Explain it to me, please."

Keep Joe talking with more questions reflecting on his remarks. Should the conversation get sidetracked and Joe's mind wanders in another direction, jerk it back on track with a "directive" question, saying, "Joe, a minute ago you said articles in the *Economist* were written by authorities. Which one impressed you the most?"

When you are in control of the conversation, try this tactic to test your skills as a communicator. Don't say a word; stay mute. Silence. People cannot tolerate silence for more than a few seconds. Usually the person answering your questions will break the silence by stuttering out a few words and you are on track again. Use silence with caution. Test it and perfect your skill to control the conversation.

Cardinal Principle 2

People Do Things for Their Reasons, Not Yours

Communicate on your listener's level, not yours. Words have meaning to people only in direct relation to their connotation. As English playwright George Bernard Shaw described the difference between British and American English: "The Americans and the British are two people separated by a common language."

During one of our great wars (that is, if you can call a war great), a directive on a British battleship regarding the storage of large shells read, "For technical reasons these warheads must be stored upside down, that is, with the bottom at the top and the top at the bottom. Now so that there shall be no misunderstanding which is the top and which is the bottom, you will notice that the top has been labeled '*Bottom*' and the bottom has been labeled '*Top.*'"

Huh!?!

To the British sailors this was readily understood. But to American sailors serving aboard the British ship, this directive was unadulterated gibberish.

The point being: in any conversation, for clarity and understanding, it is best to use words that are on your listener's level of connotation. For example, if I invited you over to my house for dinner, what time would your arrive? Noon? Six o'clock? Seven o'clock? Eight o'clock? To some people, *Dinner* is at noon and *Supper* is in the evening. To some, the evening meal is early; to others late. As a communicator, it is your job to communicate; it is not the listener's responsibility to understand what you mean. Inviting you to dinner, I should have been specific, saying, "Please join us for dinner tonight. We serve dinner at 6:00 P.M. and the cocktail hour begins at 5:00 P.M."

Cardinal Principle 3

Be Assertive, Not Aggressive

Medical-minded friends have told me that there are many facets to the human brain. The right brain is creative, intuitive, and perceptive. The left brain is logical, reasoning, and detail-oriented. A German neuropathologist named Carl Wernicke explored and discovered the part of the brain where visual and auditory memory are stored, with particular emphasis on the identification of names, persons, places, and things, in other words, "Noun," which is one of the eight different categories of the English language. About the same time Paul Boca, a French surgeon, discovered another section of the brain, the left side, which has to do with assessing and comprehending the syntax of words while listening. You might call this the action or the "Verb" side of the brain.

Another finding is that there is a shiny frontal side to the brain that makes people dynamic and aggressive. Employing this side of the brain, you can verbally duel someone to death to get your way. You may *force* someone agree with you, but without understanding what you mean. This is a no-win situation.

It is the soft understanding underside of the brain that gives you the power to gently assert yourself. The assertive side empowers you to get people to do what you want them to do, plus having them take the action because they want to—and even look forward to doing what you ask.

There are just two ways to get others to react favorably to you: by compulsion or by persuasion. Compulsion is aggressive domination. With this method you can verbally beat one into submission. This is typical of the old-school style of persuasion: "Do what I say or you are fired." This may get immediate acceptance, but over time resentment and anger fester in the mind. People do more than get mad. They scheme on how to even with you. This is a no-win situation for either party.

Gentle assertive persuasion allows you to not only get others to *agree* with you, but they *see* and understand the message you want to convey. This is a favorable solution where both sides win. There is excitement, stimulation, and energy in having a meaningful dialogue that ends in an agreeable conclusion, be it in cordial personal exchange of viewpoints or in for-profit sales presentations.

The ability to work successfully with people is the one common skill possessed by highly successful people, according to studies done by Harvard, Stanford, MIT, and think tanks. The power to persuade is critical in every human interaction. It is a natural instinct to want to influence, persuade, and motivate others to listen to us, to trust our judgment and, above all else, to like us.

Man's innermost desire is to be respected as an individual, to be appreciated and to be liked.

Are we born with the attributes of persuasion and the power to influence and motivate others? Absolutely not! These are skills to be learned and earned through, study, practice and determination to be successful. Social psychologists tell us that personality is not a divinely-inspired gift or talent. It is something that can be developed over time. Each and every one of us has the capacity to develop a winning personality with the power to persuade, influence and motivate.

The **Power to Persuade** is manifest in the ability to cause others to either change or make up their minds, to change opinions, beliefs, or ideas and to do it of their own free will—voluntarily without compulsion.

The **Power to Influence** is personal. It has to do with how you are perceived by others. How you are perceived is vital to your ability to influence people. Are you viewed as an authority? Are you credible and are you respected as being worthy of trust?

The **Power to Motivate** is the action you ask people to take. If you have earned their trust, people will generally accept and delight in taking the action you suggest.

First and foremost, to earn the ability to influence, persuade, and motivate, you must win the friendship of others. To do this, you must be friendly—you must like yourself and sincerely like other people. You must be perceived as being a friend if you want to persuade anyone to your way of thinking. People have a tendency to act favorably to any action requested by a friend. A friend is someone who we like and we like them because they seem to like us.

Each human is a unique individual. No two people are exactly alike. This unique difference is the charm and the challenge of being a winner in dealing with people. Each individual is uniquely different in attitude, ideology, background, philosophy, and perception. These are mental barriers to communication that must be pierced before there can be a meeting of minds and acceptance of ideas.

To be a winner in dealing with others, it is imperative to find out their state of mind. Are they happy and cordial or are they hurting? It is important to know their immediate state of mind and to determine their desires. People have two basic motives in life: to find happiness and to avoid pain. To persuade someone that you have the solution to their situation, you have to show them how they can get from where they are to where they want to be.

To many people, the word *persuasion* denotes being brash, forceful, overbearing and abrasive. Hack salespeople are partially responsible for this misperception. In reality, some of the very best persuaders and motivators are more prone to logic, details, specifics, and perfection.

Here is a good example of an aggressive versus assertive personality. Have you ever been caught trying to decide which one of two lines to wait in? You can be sure that Murphy's law will affect the line you select. The line stops and is held up. You selected the wrong line. It is maddening. Blood pressure shoots-up, temper flares and ugly aggression surfaces.

I watched this happen while waiting in line to exchange an airplane ticket. Murphy's Law was in effect. The line was moving at a snail's pace and one man's irritation was beginning to blossom—his hands clenched, his lips pursed as his face flushed in obvious agitation.

He barged his way to the counter, slammed his fist down with a bang and in a loud, aggressive voice he asked, "Do you know who I am?" (Obviously, he was an important customer.) The attendant, equally as aggressive, hollered to another attendant, "Hey, Sally, now we got one who doesn't know who he is." The two combined hand gestures, eye contact, and words to set in concrete the fact that the man would never fly that airline again. People don't just get mad: they get even.

Here is how an assertive personality would have handled this touchy situation. There are just four simple steps to disarm an aggressor:

1. Let the other person know that you understand how they feel, saying, "I know you are in a hurry." Reinforce the words with a disarming gesture and a submissive smile.

2. Bring the conversation back to reality by saying, " The person I am waiting on is in a hurry, too." Add emphasis by pointing to the person you are now serving.

3. Tell them what you would like them to do: "Please take your place back in line so I can finish with this customer." Add a gesture to indicate the direction by nodding your head and pointing to his position in line.

4. Finally, reward the person for doing what you ask. Point to your watch as you tell him, "This way I will be able to take care of you and you will be certain to make your flight on time."

Cardinal Principle 4

Compliment the Deed Done or Performance—
Not the Person

When you compliment a person without referring to a *Reason Why*, you risk being accused of being a phony or insincere. It is always better to give sincere and honest appreciation for a particular deed, action, or performance to which the person can relate.

When trying to compliment a person for doing a good job, do not say, "Pete, that was a great job." Be specific and say, "Pete, your report was right on the money. You must have put a lot of time and effort into the details." On the other hand, if the report was not on the money and it was not up to your expectations, how should it be handled? You might say, "Pete, this is a terrible report. Do it over." This is a "No Win" response. If the report was that far off, fire Pete, but don't ruin a working relationship.

Instead, this situation might be handled with diplomacy: "Pete, I can see you put a lot of work into this report. I'm wondering, in your research did you consider this approach (suggesting what you expected)?" This is the way a master communicator would amicably resolve the situation and, in the process, win his point and save a relationship. It is the job of the communicator to communicate.

What goes through your mind when someone tosses you a compliment? You're flattered, but there is always that element of skepticism, and you wonder to yourself, "What does he want from me? I'll bet he is going to ask for a favor." But when you receive a compliment for a job well done, you know that you have performed well and accept the kind words with a good feeling that they are well meant and not a sham.

Recently, I visited a museum with a group of friends. A docent gave our group a fascinating commentary. His knowledge and enthusiasm were contagious. At the end of the tour someone said to him, "Thank you. That was an interesting tour." His response was a dull, "Thanks." But when several members of the group demonstrated their appreciation to him, saying, "Thank you, Dave, for your delightful commentary. It made our afternoon a most enjoyable experience." A happy smile crossed his face and he returned the favor with his genuine, "Thank you all. You were a most attentive audience. You, too, made my day." This is the way you can be a winner in every interaction with others.

Cardinal Principle 5

Accentuate the Positive, Minimize the Negative

Famous songwriter and composer Johnny Mercer gave substance to this principle when he wrote these lyrics: "Accentuate the positive . . . eliminate the negative . . . don't mess with Mr. in-between." This tune was on the Hit Parade list for many years.

Teachers would do well to adhere to this positive principle. When grading tests, they concentrate on the negative. A kid misses two words on a spelling test and the test is marked in big red letters "2 Wrong," instead of "98% Correct." Kids should be taught to think positive, not negative.

This is also good advice when dealing with people. Will Rogers, the noted humorist, made the sage observation, "I never met a man I didn't like." If you want to win friends, influence others, and be successful in all your relationships with others, look for a positive winning strength in everyone you meet.

Psychologists tell us that people have a natural tendency to be friends with others who behave the same as they do. In other words, we like people who have the same likes, desires, and weaknesses that prevail in our life.

Early in history, 400 B.C. to be exact, the Senator Pericles put his finger on this human failing when he wrote: "Man can only accept the accomplishments of others when he feels that he is capable of doing the same or could do it with greater success."

Pericles was chosen, because of his wisdom and eminent reputation, to eulogize the fallen heroes of the Peloponnesian War. He stepped to the podium and let his eyes sweep across the assemblage before speaking. Then in a soft voice he spoke: "I could have wished that the reputations of many brave men would not be imperiled in the mouth of a single individual to stand or fall according as he spoke well or ill. For it is hard to speak properly on a subject where it is even difficult to convince your hearers that you are speaking the truth. On the one hand, the friend who is familiar with every fact of the story may think that some point has not been set forth with that fullness which he wishes and knows it to deserve; on the other, he who is a stranger to the matter may be led by envy to suspect exaggeration if he hears anything above his own nature."

The point is well made that men can endure to hear others

praised as long as they can persuade themselves of their own ability to equal the action. This is where envy rears its ugly head and with it incredulity sets in.

Andrew Carnegie had a positive attitude when he said, "I insist on surrounding myself with people who have talents I do not have." This is one of the reasons why he became rich, famous, and a legend.

Practice Carnegie's attitude with everyone you meet. Look for unique differences that set them apart and make them interesting to you. This way, you will reinforce and augment your own skills and abilities. This is a foundation on which you can build a happy and prosperous life. Begin today, with the very next person you meet, to build a relationship on a positive footing of respect for one another.

Cardinal Principle 6

Respond to Feelings, Not to Content

Feelings are the power generators of the human body. They are electric and carry high voltage in moving people to action. Every action, every decision, is triggered by a charge of emotion. Our *Feelers* are in command of our *Thinkers*. Whenever we make a decision, we call on our emotional "feelers" to help make up our minds; then we call on our logical "thinkers" to justify our decision.

My wife sees a gorgeous and expensive diamond bracelet she knows is way beyond our budget. But she wants it. That evil twin called "Emotion" takes control and gives her powerful reasons why she should have it:

1. She will be the envy of all her friends,
2. Everyone who sees it will think we are rich and have arrived.
3. It will look magnificent with her new dress.
4. It will make her feel good.
5. It only costs ten equal, easy payments, which we probably can afford by stretching our budget just a wee bit.

Emotions dictate the purchase. Then logic comes to her rescue. She justifies buying the bracelet when her *Thinkers* say, "Of course, diamonds are a wise investment. The bracelet will certainly appreciate in value, and the investment made in it will probably double." Sure it will???

Good communicators know the value of emotions and feelings, and know how to stroke the right chords to influence a favorable decision. Respond to feelings and you will be a winner in every personal interaction.

My daughter, Jill, came home from school one afternoon asking if she could go to the movies that evening with some friends. The following dialogue between the two of us illustrates how to respond to feelings.

Jill: Dad, all the kids are going to the movies tonight. Can I go with them?

Dad: Oh, I know you'd like to go the movies tonight, but this is Wednesday and you know the rules: 'No going out on a school night.' (If you have rules, you avoid problems.) Besides, you have homework to do.

Jill: But, Dad, all the other parents are letting their kids go!

Now at this point don't get into a parenting mode. Do not use a weak argument. Deal from strength.

Dad: I know you want to go to the movies (I'm responding to her feelings), but tomorrow's a school day.

Jill (staring me right in the eye): My homework is all done.

Dad (looking down—not directly into her eye—as this would provoke a fight): I'm glad your homework is done, but the rules are no going out on a school night.

Jill (stomping her foot): It's not fair.

Dad (nodding in her direction): I know you think it's not fair, but tomorrow is a school day.

Jill (irritated): All the other kids are going . . . I hope I don't grow up to be an old fuddy-duddy like you.

At this point an aggressive father looking for a fight might have said, "I suppose you will." And in so doing, admits that he is a mean, nasty, disagreeable old fuddy-duddy. So, instead, I respond to her feelings.,

Dad: I know you are concerned about that, but tomorrow's a school day. Stay home and review your homework.

One week later she came home from school and said, "Dad, because you made me stay home and review my homework, I got an 'A' on my test." Then she mumbled, with a tint of embarrassment, "The other kids didn't do so well."

When you respond to feelings, it shows that you appreciate and respect how the other person feels and, by so doing, that other is less likely to anger. Top-notch communicators and salespeople practice this principle. Whenever they get a negative reaction, they respond to feelings with, "I know how you *Feel*, others have *Felt* this way, too. But when they *Found* this special benefit, they *Felt* differently."

Cardinal Principle 7

Never Tell Anyone They are Wrong

Telling someone, "I don't agree with you. You're wrong" triggers a negative emotion. The quickest way to get a black eye is to hit someone else in the eye first. Anytime a negative notion is inserted into a conversation, the conversation might continue, but the communication stops. It is the job of the communicator to short-circuit the conflict and regain control.

You know you are going to get into an argument when someone says to you, "I agree with you in principle, *but.*" **But** is the spark that ignites an argument. Body language begins to surface, muscles stiffen, eyes dilate, eyebrows raise, and hackles on the back of the neck begin to bristle. Both sides gird themselves for a battle to the finish.

Think about the last time you had an argument with your spouse. If you are both type "A" personalities, your conversation shifts into drive. Try this scenario for the wrong way to handle a sticky argument:

You are upset, you bristle, and you say, "Your attitude really annoys me." And your other half gives it right back to you with, "Yeah! Well I live here, too, and I can do whatever I damned well please." From this moment on, your voices reach a new decibel rating, with the argument boiling over with yelling and screaming.

The only people who know what is going on are the neighbors who are listening and refereeing over the backyard fence. You should call the neighbors to find out who won.

The right way to short-circuit this argument would be for the person in control to say, "Honey, I'm sorry that I caused you a problem (responding to feelings). So, let's talk about it amicably so we can go on enjoying this evening together."

There is never a true winner in an argument. An aggressive personality can force agreement, but an assertive in-control communicator can help people *See and Agree* with each other.

The flip side of never telling someone they are wrong is: When you are wrong and you know you are wrong, be quick to admit your mistake. Never be stubborn and duel someone to the death defending an issue that you know is wrong. When you quickly admit your error you immediately disarm an argument and will always be a winner.

Cardinal Principle 8

Be Tactfully Honest

Honesty is being truthful and sincere, certainly an essential and noble quality. But to be brutally honest is about as tactful as a bulldozer knocking down a brick wall. Brutal honesty shatters and hurts feelings. When you are caught in a situation requiring straightforward honesty and delicate perception of the right thing to do, be tactfully honest. Be straightforward, but phrase your words delicately to avoid offending.

Words phrased differently can say the same thing but have an entirely different connotation. Two boys, Harry and Paul, were at a school dance. A young lady had chosen Harry as her dance partner. She was not the most attractive girl in the room. At the end of the dance Harry leaned over and whispered in her ear. She gave him a look that would kill, slapped him hard alongside his head, and stomped off.

Paul asked, "What did you say to that girl?" Harry replied, "I told her that she had a face that would stop a clock." Paul accused him of being brutally honest and went off to dance with the same young lady. At the end of the dance he, too, leaned over and whispered in her ear. The young lady stepped back, threw her arms around his neck, and smothered him with a big, appreciative kiss.

"What did you say to her?" Harry asked. "Same thing you said," was Paul's reply. "You told her she had a face that would stop a clock?" asked Harry. "Yes," was the answer and then Paul qualified it by saying,

"Except I was tactfully honest. I said, 'Honey, when I look at you, time stands still.'"

Both boys said the same thing, but one was brutally honest, the other tactfully honest. One boy was a "kissable" winner; the other boy was a "slapped-in-the-face" loser.

Cardinal Principle 9

There is a Purpose to All Communication and Conversation

There is a purpose to everything we do: We want *some*thing. There are just four purposes to any conversation or action we take. Before you engage your brain and open your mouth to utter your first word in any interaction with others, decide what it is you want to accomplish. Do you want to:

1. Share information
2. Instruct
3. Persuade or convince
4. Develop a mutually beneficial relationship

Don't try to mix all four together. Set one objective at a time. Before you initiate a conversation, grab control. You be the leader and decide the direction you want it to take. This is the rudder that gives direction to the conversation and carries it to a logical conclusion. When you do not have a definite purpose, the conversation wanders aimlessly and each participant wonders, "What was that conversation all about?"

Here's a conversation I had with my wife one evening. Before I divulge the answer I am going to ask you, "What objective did my wife have in her mind?"

I arrived home from work and asked my wife, "Honey, how was your day?" Here's how she responded to my question: "How was my day? It was miserable. The dishwasher won't work and I have a load of dirty dishes. *Your* dog knocked over my new lamp and I've been cleaning up the mess all day. I'm tired and don't want to cook. Will you take me out to dinner?"

Now, I'm asking, do you think she was:

1. Sharing information with me?

2. Informing me?

3. Persuading me to take her out to dinner?

Mutually beneficial relationships are built on straight talk. Get right to the point with tactful honesty. My wife had had a rough day, and her objective was to go out to dinner. Had she been more in control of the conversation, she might have said this when I asked how her day had been: "Hi, good to see you home; let's go out to dinner. I know you've had a busy day, and I would like to share mine with you."

The prime reason people do not communicate with straight talk is fear of being wrong, of being reprimanded, or of making a mistake. Tactful honesty will make you winner every time.

I have a neighbor whose young son just acquired his driver's license. His father, worried about the driving skill of the kid, put the fear of reprisal into his son's heart by telling him, "If you ever get a speeding ticket or damage the car in any way, you will be grounded. You will be confined to your room for a month. There will be no dates, no allowance, and no fun."

Three guesses what happened. If your first guess was, "The kid had an accident," you would have guessed right. Now, this kid is a tactful, straight-talking communicator. Here's how he handled telling his dad what happened:

> Good news for you, Dad! You know how you've been talking with Mom about getting a new car because the old one needs new tires and a new transmission and a new paint job? Well, Dad, the time has come. You'll be glad to know that now you can get that new Cadillac you and Mom have been wishing for. Tonight, Dad, I wrecked the old one.

What objective did this kid have in mind? You'd be right if you guessed that his objective was to prayerfully persuade Pop to be lenient with him. He accentuated the positive and minimized the negative.

Accentuate the positive. Tactful honesty. Straight talk. This is how you can be a wizard at selling yourself and communicating in the winner's circle.

Cardinal Principle 10

Play Ball

Conversation is like a baseball game. There is a pitcher and a catcher. The pitcher will talk and the catcher will listen. The subject of the conversation is the ball that is tossed back and forth as they change positions from catcher to pitcher. The objective of the pitching and catching might be a cordial and friendly exchange of information or a purposeful effort to persuade someone to change their perspective or opinion.

It is your job as the communicator to control the game. It is your job to know the mindset of the person with whom you are playing. And, knowing this, you should deliver messages that capture his attention and appeal to his mind. As you pitch words and thoughts back and forth, stay in control. Keep your objective in mind. Direct your words to play on the strengths and the weaknesses of the other person.

As a persuasive communicator, your job is to know how hard, how fast, and exactly where to deliver the message. A pitcher knows when he throws the ball it must be on target to be a winner. Wild pitches tosses go nowhere in a game of words.

Tommy Henrich, a famous right fielder for the New York Yankees, was quoted as saying in an interview, "Catching a fly ball is a pleasure, but knowing what to do with it is a business." In baseball, when a player catches a ball, he makes a split-second decision on what to do with it: Does he pitch it to first base, second base, third base, or to the catcher at home plate? There's no room for error in the big leagues, and there is similarly little room for error in important dialogues between people.

Star players in sports make big money because they know exactly what to do with the ball when they get it. You can be a big-league communicator and make big money, too, when you know where to toss the verbal ball and how to control the dialogue.

Cardinal Principle 11

Listen and Learn

Too often, people have the wrong assumption of what it takes to be a good communicator. We assume that communicating and influencing attitudes and viewpoints of other people hinges on the ability to use words and have impressive verbal skills.

The ability to speak well is important, but it is equally important to be able to listen well. The key factor to being a good listener is the ability to overestimate the value and importance of the other person's point of view. Be generous and magnanimous in respecting what the other person has to say.

Communicating requires information about the mindset of the other person. To secure this information, you must first be a good questioner. Generally in a conversation, the questions you ask are more important than what you say.

Rhetorical questions have power in grabbing the other person's immediate attention. No answer is expected from a rhetorical question. They are used for effect and to emphasize a point. Politicians use this technique when they ask, "Are you better off today than you were four years ago?" Salespeople use this tactic to drive home a sales point, saying, "What would you do if you had a paycheck guaranteed for life?"

Once you direct the question, it is essential that you be an attentive listener. The vital and most important part of communicating is the ability to listen to the other person's words. Listen attentively, using your eyes and your body as well as your ears. Let others see, feel and know that you are absorbing every word they utter.

Learn to be a good listener. When you do, you establish a solid foundation of confidence and trust. To be trusted is higher on the scale of success than to be loved. Don't talk to fill the great void of silence; let others fill the void. And, above all else, keep your ego in a jar. Only open it to stuff in more information that will make you very wise and help you build lasting relationships—in your personal life as well in business.

Rather than opening a conversation with some inane remark or a hackneyed statement that leads nowhere, ask a question of some substance.

You establish control of the conversation when you open with a question that is objective and cannot be answered 'yes' or 'no' or 'maybe.'

After the cordial exchange of 'Hello," ask for their opinion on some meaningful matter of concern. "Mike, I'm stymied. I need your candid opinion on this new product." You make people feel important when you ask for their opinion. When you make someone feel important you are taking the first step to winning a sale, an argument, or a discussion.

One morning my young daughter asked for her mother's opinion on a family matter. My wife, wanting to pass the question off to me, said, "Ann, go ask your father his opinion." To which my daughter replied, "No, Mom. I don't want to know that much about it."

Caution: if the person to whom you asked the question begins to go off on a tangent, it is your job to bring it back in focus. To do this, ask a question to direct the conversation back on your objective, saying, "A minute ago you talked about the new flower arrangement. Please expand on this and tell me more."

A Master Communicator is always in control. Never leave yourself open to relinquishing control of the dialogue. Here's an example of what can happen in a business situation:

A manager comes in to his boss' office and says, "I've got a personnel problem. Bill Jones that new member of my team, is creating dissension in my department. I don't want to fire him. *What do you think I should do about it?"*

The biggest mistake you could make would be to say, "I don't know. Let me think about it." You may be stressed, and saying this may seem to be an easy way out, but what you have just done is make his problem *your* problem. The next day your manager comes to you and asks, "Boss, what is your solution to the Bill situation?"

The right response should have been, "What do *you* think you should do about it?" Toss the ball back into his hands. Make him *think* what should be done to solve the problem. A proven technique to keep control is to answer a question with a question.

Here's how you can develop some good listening habits:

- *Button your lip and don't interrupt.* It is impossible to talk and listen at the same time. Do not utter a word until the other person is finished talking.

- *Be mentally alert.* Keep an open and receptive mind to what the other person is saying. Even if you mentally disagree, keep an open mind.

- *Listen for thoughts, not words.* Focus your mind on what is being said. Shut out all distractions to absorbing what is being said to you.

- *"Oh-yes-I-see-what-you-mean" interjections.* This lets the other person know you are listening, intently. Augment this with body gestures like nodding your head in agreement.

- *Listen for ideas.* How does the other person say things? Do the words flow smoothly together or do they ramble. Listen for these overtones and you will be in control of the conversation.

- *Practice listening.* Practice to perfect your listening skills. Sharpen your listening skills by practicing on everyone you meet: your friends, your family, and your associates.

- *Ponder your answers.* When you are asked a question, do not leap immediately into a response. Pause long enough to let it be known that you are giving serious and considered thought to your answer.

Cardinal Principle 12

Create a Positive Personal Attitude

What kind of a person are you? Behavioral psychologists classify personality types as:

- Type A if you are outgoing, sociable, self-confident, and uninhibited in associating with other people.

- Type B if you are calm and laid back, logical and analytical in your thinking.

- A blend of both A and B, which is a positive combination for a salesperson.

When you recognize your own temperament and can classify the temperament of the person to whom you are speaking, you are well equipped to exercise positive control of any conversation.

Always create a positive attitude when meeting with people for the first time. Try to make a good, positive first impression. The old saying is true: You never get a second chance to make a first impression.

As individuals, people are, for the most part, unsolvable puzzles.

All people are born different. No two are exactly alike. We all think differently. Every individual is motivated and stimulated by different stimuli. This is one of the most fascinating and challenging aspects of being a communicator. Carl Jung, a Swiss psychologist of the 1900s, introduced the concept of introvert and extrovert (a different identification of the Type A and Type B personalities). He claimed that faced with the same exact situation, each of us would have a distinctively different way of responding and getting the job done.

The problem is that that most people suffer through life never capitalizing on their own abilities. As a result they waste their time on small tasks and never achieve their full potential. Not to believe in yourself or to recognize your own personality traits is a tragedy that stifles a lifetime of achievement.

In 1912, Harry Leon Wilson wrote a 300-page novel entitled *Bunker Bean.* This is a fascinating story about a man who suffered through his life in poverty and despair until he was tricked into believing in himself.

Bunker Bean, as a child, was left alone in the world. He lived timidly, people bullied him and his mind was full of fears and doubts. He always wished he could be different. He knew that he was inferior to his contemporaries. He didn't like his name; he was too short; he wasn't handsome; he didn't have nice clothes. He was afraid of life. He was even afraid of himself.

Then one day Bunker met a shrewd and false spiritualistic medium who persuaded him to believe in the power of reincarnation. In return for a substantial amount of money, the medium could tell Bunker what he had been in his previous life.

Bunker was delighted to learn that he, the weak and timid soul, had once been the great Napoleon Bonaparte and that the karma of Napoleon was just now entering the life of Bunker.

Bunker looked at himself in the mirror and agreed that there was certain majesty in his appearance. He vibrated with this new fresh power and became contemptuous of the fears that had terrorized his other life. Napoleon believed in himself and now Bunker was beginning to believe in himself, too.

Bunker was now a different person and other people began to notice the change. At work he was given more important assignments and a raise in salary.

Then he was struck by another thought: Who had he been before he was Napoleon?" Once again he contacted the medium. Money was no obstacle. He could pay well for the information.

Bunker learned to his delight that before he was born as Napoleon he had been the great Egyptian Pharaoh Ramses. As Ramses he had been tall and handsome, so he hired the best tailors and dressed the part.

Power flowed through him from his mental images of the kingly demeanor of the Pharaoh and how he had led victorious armies as Napoleon. He thought courage at night and awoke in the morning with a giant's strength.

Then one day Bunker discovered that the medium was a fake. He had been cheated and bilked out his money. Bunker realized he had not been a king or an emperor.

But in the years that Bunker had believed he was a king and a conqueror, he had formed the habits that go with success. He had learned a great truth: "That believing in yourself is all that matters." Over the years he had lived the myth of imagining that he was great. He had earned wealth, power and prestige. Ramses and Napoleon had only been crude bits of scaffolding on which he had climbed to success. Every man is born to riches. To believe is all that matters.

Now that you have read Bunker Bean's story, ask yourself, "What kind of person am I now and what kind of person do I want to be?" When you decide, go through the motions of being that person you feel you are meant to become, then "Fake it 'til you make it."

A Bonus Cardinal Principle

A Baker's Dozen

This is something extra, the frosting on the cake. The term *a baker's dozen* originated when certain foods were ordered by the dozen. Order a dozen donuts, and one bonus donut was tossed in to ensure good customer relations. The Chinese have a similar term, *cumshaw*, which means "something extra." Here's how you can add something "extra" to your karma and be a winner as a communicator.

Write the letter you don't have to write. Take time to compliment, congratulate, or recognize the accomplishment of a deserving friend, colleague, or acquaintance.

Compliment generously and honestly. Look carefully and you will find something nice to say to everyone you meet. Abe Lincoln personified this principle when he wrote, "an ounce of honey is better than a pound of gall." Start the conversation with the very next man or woman you meet with a compliment. Everybody has a positive that warrants recognition. Look for it and you'll find it.

Edgar Guest, one of the great poets, wrote a wonderful poem about complimenting others. It is called *Tomorrow.*

Tomorrow

He was going to be all that a mortal should be
    Tomorrow.
No one should be kinder or braver than he
    Tomorrow.
A friend who was troubled and weary he knew,
Who'd be glad of a lift and needed it, too
On him he would call to see what he could do
    Tomorrow.

Each morning he stacked up the letter he'd write
    Tomorrow.
And thought of the folk he would fill with delight
    Tomorrow.
It was too bad, indeed, he was busy today,
And hadn't a minute to stop on his way;
More time he would have to give to others, he'd say
    Tomorrow.

The greatest of workers this man would have been
    Tomorrow
The world would have known him, had he ever seen tomorrow
But the fact is, he died and faded from view,
And all that he left when he was through
Was a mountain of things he intended to do
    Tomorrow.

For the next thirty days practice being nice to everyone you meet. Set your mind to do this consciously and soon you will be complimenting people subconsciously. This is the first step to making you a winner in dealing with people.

7 Words Have Power— Use Them *Right* and Be a Winner

A word is the most powerful drug used by mankind.

—Rudyard Kipling

There is at least one accomplishment that presents a great scientific puzzle. It is central to the success of our species, yet we have only a rudimentary understanding of how it may have evolved and how it works as a system. Despite that, we do it so effortlessly.

That accomplishment-puzzle is *language*.

Roughly a quarter of a million years ago man discovered the power to utter sounds. This was about the time man stopped using his mouth to bite, fight, and grub for food (though that mouth is still used to deliver biting remarks and is often a receptacle in which to put one's foot).

But from time to time the mouth utters words that result in meaningful conversation.

Our challenge is how to effectively use our mouth in cooperation with our brain to communicate with each other to:

- Be understood
- Get compliance
- Achieve cooperation
- Fine-tune relationships
- Earn trust and loyalty

Our language comes alive through the use of vivid, picturesque, and powerful words. The right words, when chosen carefully, are charged with high-voltage electricity that engages emotions, stirs the senses, opens the window of the mind to release stored memories, and creates reality.

I have studied the lives of dynamic leaders who have made a difference in history. The one common denominator is their ability to use words that vibrate with energy and make historical events come alive. Leaders are remembered more for what they have said than for what they have done. One person in history who ran counter to this truism was Napoleon Bonaparte. His fame was due to his deeds, not his words. However, he must have possessed a mastery of words to stir men's minds to action because he transformed his demoralized, starving troops into an invincible army. He must have prodded the minds of his troops with words of fame and glory. His final act while in dreary exile at Saint Helena was to write his memoirs. History does remember him for his deeds, but also for his winning words when he wrote, "Small plans do not inflame the hearts of men." His bold plans of conquest and empire did indeed inflame the hearts of the men in his army.

Consider the people whose powerful words have stimulated men's minds to action and in the process made or changed the course of history:

Thomas Jefferson in the Declaration of Independence wrote words that compelled men to risk their lives, their fortunes, and their sacred honor.

President Franklin Delano Roosevelt's personal "Fireside Chats" mesmerized people as they listened to their radios and he relieved their fears by counseling in his Inaugural Address, "The only thing we have to fear is fear itself."

President John F. Kennedy challenged a nation with his, "Ask not what your country can do for you. Ask what you can do for your country."

President Abraham Lincoln stirred listeners as he spoke of "A government of, by and for the people."

Both Kennedy's and Lincoln's pronouncements are words lifted from an oration given by the Greek statesman Pericles about 400 B.C.

> Martin Luther King, one of the great orators of the twentieth century, transformed our nation with his "I Have A Dream" speech. He began his speech in the first person, present tense. Then gradually and with great skill he led every listener into his message: "*We* shall overcome."
>
> Sir Winston Churchill's most famous speech of all, "I have nothing to offer but *blood, toil, tears* and *sweat*" (also first uttered by Pericles) was delivered the first person, present tense. Into his fabric of words, he wove the British people, the righteousness of God, and the glory of the British Empire.

Winston Churchill, British statesman and prime minister during World War II, was noted for his mastery of words and his use of the English language. In the darkest days, the likelihood of England's winning the war was in serious doubt. Sir Winston rallied his people by using the dynamic power of words.

History (through news correspondent Edward R. Murrow) recorded that, "Sir Winston mobilized the English language and sent it into battle." Churchill had a mastery of the English language. He was a master communicator. He knew how to assemble the power of high-voltage words to generate positive action. He hurled words of defiance at Germany and offered inspirational words of victory to the English people in this famous speech to the House of Commons after he was named Prime Minister at the beginning of World War II.:

> I have nothing to offer but blood, toil, tears and sweat. You ask, what is our policy? I can say, it is to wage war by sea, land and air with all the might and with all the strength that God can give us; to wage war against a monstrous tyranny, never surpassed in the dark, lamentable catalogue of human crime. That is our policy. You ask, what is our aim? I can answer in one word: It is victory, victory at all costs, victory in spite of all the terror, victory no matter how long and hard the road may be; for without victory, there is no survival. Let that be realized; no survival for the British Empire, no survival for all that the British Empire has stood for. But I take up my task with buoyancy and hope. Come then, let us go forward

together with our united strength. We shall go to the end, we shall fight in France, we shall fight on the seas and oceans, we shall fight with growing confidence and strength in the air, we shall defend our island, whatever the cost may be. We shall fight on the beaches, we shall fight on the landing grounds, we shall fight in the fields and in the streets, and we shall fight in the hills. We shall never surrender.

The words you use have positive and negative power. Words can make friends or enemies. Words can start a good personal relationship or end it. Sweet and affectionate words can begin a love affair. Sharp and ugly words can end the love affair. Words start wars, and words end wars.

Words can take on unintended imagery to influence people's actions in bizarre and unintended ways. In some cases word usage can be constructed to create a purposeful distorted image. Cardinal Richelieu, French statesman and prelate under Louis XIII, said, "Give me the innocent statements of ten honest men and I will turn them into lies." Editors, publishers, and reporters want to provide unusual news or report big stories to capture their reader's attention and to fulfill their own ambitions. (This may be the goal of tabloids and news organizations that are more "entertainment" than news, but there are still many in journalism and publishing working for the public good.)

Words have power. There is the story told about the Sultan who, fretting over his mortality, called on a seer to predict his destiny. The prophet, after consulting with the gods, said, "Sire, you will live to see all your family dead." The startled Sultan, not liking the pronouncement, immediately called for his executioner. The next day the Sultan called on a wiser prophet who, after chatting with the gods, prophesied, "Sire, you are blessed with long life, and you will outlive all your family." The Sultan was so delighted with the good tidings that he gave the "wiser" prophet his prized and favorite elephant.

Both prophets predicted the same result, but the wiser of the two knew the magic power of words to convey a positive, not a negative, message. Words, when used properly, have power. They can dress up an idea so that it flows into the mind smoothly, softly, and silently without obstruction.

Master communicators, master persuaders, winners in making friends and influencing others and earning money, practice and perfect the magic of using words to win their way. We can credit the Anglo-Saxons for their contribution of simple single-syllable words.

The English language was born in the year 1066. This was the year William, the Duke of Normandy, better known as William the Conqueror, defeated King Harold of Hastings and the French occupied England. Of course, William was French and only spoke French. (And of course Latin, which was the official language of courts and intellectual life.) He could have imposed the French language on England, but he elected not to. Had he done so, I would be writing this book in French instead of English.

But like the Roman general Caesar before him, William reasoned, "Who would want the God-forsaken island called England? It has a damp, lousy climate and is inhabited by dirty-smelling peasants who speak nothing but harsh, rasping Anglo-Saxon German."

The French soldiers are the ones responsible for the English language. And sex played a major role. French soldiers fell in love with the Anglo-Saxon women whose husbands had been killed in the war. These men wanted to marry the women and stay in England, but first they had to get permission from France, which was willingly granted. But there was one hitch. The French soldiers wanted to teach them French. The French government under King Henry 1 said, "Absolutely not. You will not teach those Anglo-Saxon women our glorious and romantic French language."

So the French soldiers countered with, "Then we will have to learn to speak Anglo-Saxon." Again the soldiers were rebuffed. They were told, "You speak the beautiful French language. Your wife will speak the raspy Anglo-Saxon." This is exactly what happened. The French dumped all of their French on top of the Anglo-Saxon German. The majority of the words in the English language are single-syllable Anglo-Saxon words, like *sweat, ask, see, deer.* Compare these same words to the multisyllable French words. *Sweat* becomes *perspire, ask* becomes *interrogate, see* becomes *perceive,* and *deer* becomes *venison.* Similarly, *sheep* becomes *mutton,* stool becomes chair .

There is a time and purpose for everything. Imagine with me that you are ordering dinner in a fancy five-star restaurant and you see on the menu, *Deer—$39.95.* You might say, "No way." But if the more sophisticated-sounding *Venison—$39.95* were offered, perhaps you would consider it. Both words convey the same message, but one has a higher-value perception, and in most cases perception is reality.

The English language has been a reservoir into which unique words flow from other languages around the world—*cul-de-sac* from French, *cumshaw* from Chinese, *lariat* from Spanish, *keiretsu* from Japanese (meaning shared destiny), *luau* from Hawaiian—to name just a few. English-speaking people never should be caught at a loss for words.

Unfortunately, we rarely put this large selection of words at our disposal to good use. Educators tell us that the average college graduate has an understanding of 10,000 words, but in the daily intercourse of conversation people only use an average of 300 to 400 words to convey their thoughts. Little wonder that we humans have a tough time communicating with each other!

Our communications are handicapped because we don't select the right word to convey the meaning we really want to convey. We fall back on tired, old colorless words that deliver unclear and confusing images. And in so doing, we confuse the clarity and miss the point of what we want to say.

It is easy to fall back on using only the few words you are accustomed to using over and over again. Do this and you are a machine. You are making acceptable noises out of your mouth, but your brain is not engaged fully to successfully communicate your thoughts to whoever is listening. I compare this to attending a church service where I am not knowledgeable about the scriptural ritual or dogma. I sing the hymns and recite the communal reading. I don't understand what I am saying, but I get a nice warm feeling for having said it.

The purpose of all conversation is to communicate—to get compliance, cooperation, agreement, and acceptance—and to be understood. It is also called salesmanship.

George Orwell, the British writer on politics and the English language and the author of *Animal Farm* and *1984*, wrote an essay entitled "Politics and the English Language." You can find it on the Internet, and I recommend it to anyone who wants to improve his/her skills as a communicator—both written and oral. Here are Orwell's "Rules you can rely on when instinct fails":

1. *Never use a metaphor, simile, or other form of speech that you are used to seeing in print.* He defines dying metaphors as "*stand shoulder-to-shoulder*," "*grist to the mill*," " *toe the line*"—all overused and twisted out of their original meaning.

   Newly invented metaphors can assist thought and paint visual images in the mind. I heard a descriptive metaphor in a speech. The speaker referred to the money in a man's wallet as " . . . stuffed fuller than a pastrami sandwich in a New York deli."

2. *Never use a long word where a short one will do.*

   Single-syllable words travel uninterrupted from the larynx to the brain. They are common, simple to identify, and used in everyday conversation. It is not that your audience does not understand multisyllabic words, but long words require slower translation and often lead to distortion of the meaning. It is your job as a communicator to communicate. It is your responsibility to tailor the words you use to the comprehension level of the person to whom you are speaking.

   H. Phelps Gates, noted American writer and author wrote four pages in which he never used a word with more than one syllable in it. Here is the last paragraph:

   > Scan the best sales job in print and you will find them rich in short words that tease the taste, make glad the eye, whet the nose and please the ear. There's nip, twang, bite and tang in short sales words. They're sweet and sour, tart or dry as the need may be. There are words like the feel of swan's down, words with a smell like smoke, cheese, mint and rose—all of them good sales tools, yet, oft as not, we'll force the use of some long, hard word and, along with it, blunt the keen edge and dull the sharp point in what we want to say.

In this one paragraph Gates used sensory metaphors to paint images and to touch feelings. Allstate Insurance does this aptly with its famous "You're in good hands" slogan. The logo is a pair of hands with palms extended. The message conveyed is,

"You are in good hands. We are here to protect and insure your interests."

3. *If it is possible to cut a word out, always cut it out.*

This is called the economy of words. Calvin Coolidge was possibly the only politician ever noted for his brevity of speech. Called "Silent Cal," the thirtieth president of the United States was known for his New England simplicity, honesty, and brevity. He said what he meant by using the barest essential words. One evening at a dinner, one of the guests offered to bet "Silent Cal" she could entice him to say more than three words. He responded, saying, "You Lose." This is still considered to be one of the great classic stories about remarks made by presidents.

Speaking as well as writing is a form of communication, and simply enough, the most effective speaking, as well as writing, is clear and concise. That is why Master Communicators continually strive for precise expression and economy of language by using the exact word to express their meaning—so they can become Master Persuaders. To do this, your dictionary should be indispensable to you. Make it your constant companion.

4. *Never use the passive where you can use the active voice.*

In speaking, the active voice is more direct and gives greater emphasis to your words. Let your words give a sense of "it's happening now." Do not say, "Mary was hit by the car." Rather, give immediacy to the words by saying, "The car hit Mary." Lace your conversation with verbs to give zest and vitality to your message. Verbs tell us what action is occurring and when it is occurring. And speak in the first person: *I, we.* All of these underscore one important point: be as direct and active in your statements as possible.

5. *Never use a foreign phrase, a scientific word or a jargon word* if you can think of an everyday English equivalent.

6. *Break any of these rules sooner than say anything outright barbarous.*

Words are electric. They are the high-voltage of all communications and selling. They are charged with energy and, when properly used, can open the window of the mind to persuade and move people to action. Successful communicators and salespeople who earn top dollars have mastered the art of using words to win their way.

Words paint mental pictures on the canvas of the mind. A word conveys no meaning until it is transformed into a picture in the mind. If I were to say to you, *tack-sa-mycket,* you would scratch your head and wonder what I was talking about. But if you were Swedish, you would instantly light up to the words *thank you.*

The magic of being a communicator is the ability to use words with skill and conviction. If you want to be a winner in dealing with people, develop a toolbox full of words. Then play with these words. Have fun changing their order to emphasize, add color, and give variety to your conversation. Don't fuss about grammar. Don't flout the rules of grammar, but don't be a slave to them.

Your job as a communicator is to communicate. Often the use of colloquial Anglo-Saxon words makes your point and gets to the action with rapier speed. Short words and old words that everyone knows the meaning of are the best to penetrate your listener's mind without interrupting the thought.

If you are trying to persuade or convince someone to your way of thinking, the right words can capture the emotions and favorably spark the imagination. There are words that can blunt the hard edge of persuasion and soften the "Being Sold" feeling. Words can either make someone feel like he is *Buying* instead of being *Sold.* The difference is significant: Feeling that I am being "Sold a Bill of Goods" is adversarial and causes one to recoil. People need to have the feeling of "I am in control. I am making my own buying decision without coercion."

Each person has his or her own unique communication style. Your style reflects your unique circumstances and personal characteristics— education, skills, experience, physical features, and moral attitudes. Whether or not you think so, you are a communicator. Every waking moment you are sharing a dialogue with everyone you meet. It might be an exchange of pleasantries, a conflict of opinion, or persuading someone to your way of thinking. You are a communicator. The question is, are you a good one? Are you liked? Are you trusted? Do others respect you and listen to your point of view, whether or not they agree with what you say? Are you a winner in dealing with people? Do you have fun in every discourse with others, regardless of winning or losing?

You can be a winner in dealing with people.

According to Webster:

Communication is the act of giving, sharing, exchanging information by talking, writing, and making gestures.

Selling is to give, deliver or exchange property, goods, or services in exchange for money or its equivalent.

Both disciplines are the same, with one exception: Selling is in exchange for money. When you are communicating, you are selling; and when you are selling, you are communicating.

So, how do you communicate so you are understood? How do you sell ideas, thoughts, products, and services that are mutually beneficial? How can you be a winner in your interpersonal relationships?

Words are the tools of the communicator. Words are the silver bullets that challenge the imagination, engage the mind and capture emotions. Everyone has a "hot button" that triggers an action. And when the right words are used, they spark the flame that ignites the desire to comply. Emotion is always in control over logic. People make decisions based on their emotional reaction, and then they call on logic to rationalize the "wisdom" of their decision.

When speaking, master communicators keep their objective in sight, but focus on the interests of the person they are speaking to. How do you find this point of interest or hot button? The wise speaker will ask objective questions and then sit back and listen as the responder reveals his innermost thoughts.

A medical doctor friend of mine is recognized in the local medical profession for his uncanny ability to accurately diagnose patients' ailments. One day in idle conversation I asked, "Ray, what is your secret? How do you do it?" The good doctor looked at me over the top of his reading glasses that were perched on the end of his nose and said, "It's not me. It's the patients. They know where they hurt. I just keep asking probing questions until I get the right answers."

Many volumes have been written about how to influence and persuade others to reveal their thoughts and innermost feelings to you. There really isn't any wrong way. Emily Post, the etiquette expert, was asked by a young man, "What is the right way to ask my girlfriend to marry me?" Emily replied, "There ain't no wrong way." It's the same with getting people to talk. Many times the very best way is *just ask*. Just asking works where you don't have the power. Or, you may have the power, but don't want to use it. Just asking works in more situations than you might think. One simple secret is to ask, "I need your help. What is your opinion on. . . . " This is a sure-fire way to get people to spill their innards to you.

Here are some words that pack power. Put them in your verbal toolbox. Adapt these words to your individual style to match your personality and the situation.

The Name. The most personal and cherished word is a person's name, particularly when it is pronounced correctly. If there is any doubt as to the correct pronunciation or spelling, ask. This shows your interest and respect. The use of the first name in most situations is acceptable. However, in higher-level, more formal situations, if the person is not known, it is wise to use only the last name—with, of course, the proper prefix (Mr., Miss, Mrs., Ms, or professional title).

Be careful not to overdo the use of the name. It is appropriate at the beginning and end of a conversation or at a time when an important point is being made, such as, "This program will insure you a paycheck for the rest of your life, Eric." This use of the name would personalize the point and cinch it securely in the mind.

A prisoner named Rafael Maestroziani escaped from a California prison. He was on the loose for several weeks. As the police and the media followed him across several states, the TV and newspapers reported his sightings. They misspelled, mispronounced, and mutilated his name. Irritated by the constant abuse of his name, Rafael took direct action. He called the TV station and complained about how they were butchering his name. He then told the news anchor exactly how his name should be pronounced. You guessed right: The police traced his call, and Rafael is once again behind bars. But his name was pronounced correctly!

Hello. This is a cordial greeting or a response too seldom used. To develop this habit of cordiality, I suggest you try this greeting on everyone you meet for the next thirty days. As you walk down the street, make it a point to give every stranger a knowing glance and then a cheery "hello." Then watch for the element of amazement, surprise, and astonishment your greeting brings. I guarantee that you will get a nod and a responsive smile in return. This is just an innocent and simple way for you to begin to develop a winning attitude. After all, it doesn't cost you anything and you have nothing to lose. For the next thirty days, give it a try. You'll be amazed at the response.

Please. This is a common courtesy word that has power in taking the bite out of a command or to dull the sharp edge off a reprimand. Prefacing a request with the word *please* makes for a pleasant obligation instead of an onerous task. The word *please* is a friendly and a common courtesy that becomes friendly persuasion: "*Please* join us for dinner tonight." One of our renowned Army generals, Omar Bradley, prefaced every command with the word *Please.*

Thank you. These two powerful words show and express gratitude and appreciation. These words are easy to say but too often omitted in everyday conversation, such as in cordial amenities like, "*Thank you,* Jim, for asking about my son."

Because. There is authority in this word because its power is that a "Reason Why" must follow it: "It is important *because* you will make more money by investing now."

If you are like I am (like me). The power of this phrase is that the word *you* must follow: "If you are like me, *you* will discover the benefit in just three days."

Might & maybe. These words soften the rough edge of persuasion. They gently leave a feeling of "I am in control." "Joe, you *might* want to consider this point." "*Maybe* you will find something special you *might* like."

You know. This gives credit to people for knowing something that they may know absolutely nothing about. The power of *you know* is that it gently strokes the ego: "Mike, I'm certain *you know* something about this. . . . "

Tell you. This is something with which the other person cannot disagree: "I could *tell you* not to worry, but I know you will." "I shouldn't *tell you* this, but you'll find out anyway."

Sharing secrets. You earn trust and get attention when you reveal something that is private knowledge: "*I shouldn't share this with you,* but, off the record, you should know. . . . "

An obvious fact. A common accepted truism is something that all can agree with. This gets people into a "yes" frame of mind: "Taxes are too high." "Gas prices are out of sight."

Don't. This is a contraction that softens the bite of "do not" and can leave a disarming impression: "Mike, *don't* feel that you have to buy this today."

Feel/felt/found. A solid way to counter an objection: "I know how you *feel* about buying now, other customers have *felt* the same as you, but when they *found* that it paid high dividends they changed their mind.

Limited quantity. When things are perceived to be in short supply, these words give a perception of value and exclusivity. To be told, "Only one to a customer," or "Limited supply," or "Only 5 left in stock," generates a competitive challenge and a sense of urgency: "I'd better get mine before someone else beats me to the value."

Which. Always give a choice between something and something instead of a choice between something and nothing. When you are asked, "*Which* color do you prefer, red or blue?" it is impossible for you to answer no. It is imperative that you identify your choice and in so doing to indicate a preference that opens the door to making a sale.

If. This is a word that assumes without a definite commitment: "*If* you were going to buy today, which one would you choose?"

If and when. Use these words carefully. "*If* you finish this report . . . " *If* is negative and implies it will not be finished. A positive way would be to say, "*When* you finish this report . . . "

Now. This can give immediacy to a decision. Always follow with a "Reason Why": "*Now* is the best time to buy because. . . . " "Do it *now* and enjoy the pleasure today."

Let's. Let's is a contraction that suggest working together to solve a problem: "Let's work this out . . . " or "Let's get together and work out the details. . . . "

Imagine. The mind thinks in pictures, and a person colors his mind's picture with his own imagination. You might say to someone, "*Imagine you have a lifetime income. What pleasures would you enjoy?*"

How to. Telling people how to accomplish something, "How to be successful" is much more powerful than "The rules of success."

Other words similarly pack punch and power. "Self-interest" words capture people's attention—words like: *How To, Wanted, Yours, Why, What, and Free*. Words that imply "News" grab attention: *Announcing, Discover, At Last, Finally* and *New*.

Words are fun to play with. Changing the order in which you place words can be an attention grabber to emphasize a thought or an idea. Take the sentence, "We crept to the window quietly, like thieves." To make the point "Quietly," you would structure your words this way, "Quietly, like thieves, we crept to the window." These changes in word order not only add emphasis, but they also add color and variety to writing and to speaking.

The real power of words is that they stroke the strings of the emotions. Vivid words paint visual images on the brain. A word has no meaning until it is coupled to a mental image. If the meaning of a word is not known, it does not produce an image in the mind. A hi-tech screening device is strategically located in the brain. This is where the words we hear are translated into mental images in the mind.

A word only has meaning when it is associated with a mental image. The brain has a hi-tech selective screening capacity that accepts and filters out word phrases or clauses that are not relevant. It gives interest and attention only to ideas of special interest. It perceives the benefit based on the personal value. And the brain retains and remembers those ideas of immediate importance.

Words are like music. When orchestrated, they have rhythm, cadence, and rhyme, and they come together like a symphony. Like all great music, once you hear it and are touched, it keeps resurfacing in your mind. It is the same with words: when carefully chosen, they break through all the clutter in the mind. They keep interrupting and sticking in the mind commanding action.

Cosmology, the study of the galaxies in outer space, is a favorite hobby of mine. At a luncheon I had the pleasure of sitting next to Carl Sagan, astronomer, writer, and renowned scientist. How to converse with a man of his intellect was the first thought that popped into my mind. Wanting to start a conversation, I boldly and provocatively stated, "Carl, I'm in the same business as you."

Then I waited to see his reaction. His brow wrinkled as he looked at me and asked, "You're an astronomer?" At least I had a conversation under way. I replied back to him, "Well, no, Carl, I'm not." Then I was quick to add, "But I believe we are exploring the same void. You are searching the heavens trying to discover the window in the black holes of space that you call singularities. Well, Carl, I am in sales and advertising. I, too, am exploring the unknown:—man's mind. I am trying to find the window in man's mind through which I can communicate intelligently." Carl talked and I listened intently.

Load your mental toolbox with words and become a master communicator. You'll have the time of your life playing with words and experimenting with their power to persuade people to agree, reply and respect you for being a master communicator. You'll discover that the challenge will be fun and financially rewarding for you.

8 Body Language, the "Sidekick" to Words

93% of all communication is nonverbal.

—Dr. Albert Mehrabian

According to Dr. Albert Mehrabian, a leading expert in nonverbal communication, words account for only 7 percent of our impact on others; tone of voice accounts for 38 percent, and facial expression accounts for 55 percent.

This might explain a comment my daughter made to me one night. I arrived home one evening and was greeted in a very quizzically and teasing way with, "Hi, Dad, how do you feel?" I was feeling in top form and responded to her, "I feel great. Why do you ask?" Her reply was, "If you feel so good, Dad, you should notify your face."

Of all the things you wear, your facial expression is the most important.

To be a winner in dealing with people, Master Communicators have learned how to use their bodies to give emphasis to their words. In tandem with this is the ability to listen to and decipher the body language of the speaker.

Words are not enough to assert your desires. Your body language must reinforce the message. Words gain power when coupled with body language. The words are the hero and body language is the sidekick/buddy who tags along to give support and emphasis.

Here are some very simple and primary body language essentials:

Body language and eye contact. Contrary to popular belief, unrelenting eye contact can be very disturbing and intimidating. We have been taught that eyes locked together places the dominant person in control. Not so, according to body language experts. They do not recommend staring the other person down: it is intimidating and confers no status on either person.

Too-intense eye contact is an invitation to fight. A good example is to watch two dogs approach each other: Their eyes are locked in contact, ears are flattened against the head, and teeth are bared.

The U.S. Forestry Services publishes a booklet for hikers and campers in bear country. Among all the cautions one critical caveat is, "Do not stare directly into the bear's eyes. This is an invitation for the bear to attack."

I have been in the great out-of-doors many times and have confronted a wide variety of wild animals, grizzly bears included. Only once in my life was I close enough to a bear to even think about starring it straight in the eye.

I was tramping along a trail in Yellowstone National Park enjoying the beautiful scenery, oblivious to the rest of the world. I stole a quick glance at the trail ahead, and there it was, a huge grizzly bear standing in my way. I had read the instructions on what to do if confronted with a grizzly, so I looked over the bear's head, stood as tall as I could stretch, made loud noises, waved my arms high above my head, and slowly backed away. I won. The bear turned and ran. I shudder to think what might have been the result had I looked the bear straight in the eye.

In popular belief it is often thought that the weaker person would break unrelenting eye contact first. Not so, according to Dr. Allan Mazur, professor of sociology. The person of higher status or the dominant personality will break eye contact first. The dominant person knows he is in control and does not want to incite any negative reaction.

The expression "to see *eye to eye*" is often misused to mean being of one mind or to think alike. Not so. The words initially had a biblical connotation of seeing eye to eye with the Lord.

Body language experts suggest the proper way to position your eyes in any conversation is to fix your glance on the forehead or a position to the side of the head. This gives the appearance of undivided attention and interest in what is being said without intimidation.

When greeting foreigners or one another, Asian people bow in deference, avoiding eye contact, arms extended and palms open in a gesture of "no weapon, we come in peace." Most pictures of Christ show him in long, flowing robes with his arms extended outward and his palms open to the viewer.

Boundaries. The arrangement of office furniture often marks a territory and conveys the warning: *Enter only when invited to do so.* Desk arrangement can form a barrier between managers and their visitors. Stop and notice in any workplace how people enter the boss's office. Low-status individuals tend to stop just inside the office door and wait to be invited in. Medium-status people walk part way in and wait for recognition. Equal-status people walk straight in and speak before they are spoken to.

This status recognition is manifest in our daily social or business contacts, too. We give deference to people whom we acknowledge or respect as being a step above us. But, if we feel equal or superior to the other person, we make joyful noises when we meet. We shake hands and are generous with our recognition. If a member of the opposite sex is involved, and it is appropriate, a kiss or a peck on the cheek will accompany the hug or the handshake.

People are just like the animals (or maybe it is the other way around). Go to the zoo someday and notice how the monkeys and chimpanzees greet each other: They embrace, kiss, shake hands, hug, and make joyful noises. A friend of mine is an anthropologist for the local zoo. He tells me that he positively believes the monkeys look forward to Sundays so they can see all the funny antics of the human visitors.

The lack or omission of friendly greetings can very subtly demoralize people because it sends a sense of not belonging or lack of recognition as an individual. Parting rituals are important, too, such as a friendly and cheerful "goodbye," "good to see you," or "see you tomorrow." Even such gestures as touching an arm, a friendly handshake, or simply looking up and nodding a pleasant "see you later" can be powerful rapport-builders.

Such seemingly insignificant actions do have a cumulative effect, making people eager to see you again and willing to comply with you.

Today, business and professional people recognize the need for recognition of employees from the bottom-up—from the delivery man to the highest executive. Individual recognition and assuring the employee feels that "*My job is important to the company and I am an important individual,*" is the key that makes employees work in harmony. The by-product of fully acknowledged communication from the bottom-up is that it relates directly to bottom-line profit.

Touch. Touching is a form of quasi-courtship that can liven any relationship if not carried too far. A gentle touch on the arm can mean many things. It says, "I like you; we are in this together," or "Let's communicate and share information." Friendship and camaraderie, not to mention love, would be pale without touching.

Teamwork and cooperation are supported and reinforced by touching. Watch the players in any sport: Every group activity is accompanied by some individual body action—the players hug and slap each other on the butt, pound on each others' helmets, and in some of the more violent sports, they body-slam each other and display semi-violent actions to signal superiority, camaraderie, and victory.

However, some forms of touching can convey extremely negative messages. For example, a touch accompanied by a verbal putdown (such as touching someone's stomach while saying, "Putting on a few pounds, huh?") doubles the intensity of the insult.

How to know whether or not touching is appropriate? If you reach out to touch someone, even though in a friendly way, and receive an icy stare or a backing off, the intended warmth turns to embarrassment. Stop, immediately.

In general, it is safe to touch others only when you establish rapport and they display "open" body language indicating they are willing to accept the touch. One caution: Take care not to overdo it or to be too effusive, especially with members of the opposite sex.

Your facial expression can be worth a thousand words or none at all. Uninhibited body language never lies. So if you want to tell about your feelings and your mental attitude, just be yourself. Anger, fear, hurt, disgust, rejection, and all sorts of negative emotions will burst open to display your inner self.

There are times when it is wise for you to avoid expressing the inner, unvarnished truth. From early childhood we have learned to suppress our body language and emotions. If we whine or cry, there will be no television tonight.

In some business negotiations, it is wise to guard the truth within yourself and learn to exhibit the deadpan expression so that you do not prematurely tip your hand. This is a talent you learn from childhood, but if you are not confident in your ability to deadpan it, you can refine your skills by learning and playing the game of poker. Although the game does involve both luck and skill, poker is primarily a game of bluffing; that is, hiding your elation for having a winning hand, signaling your disappointment for holding a mediocre hand, or raising your eyebrows or frowning to telegraph your hopes and expectations that the cards to come will favor you.

A friend of mine taught his dog how to play poker. It was a sight to behold, watching that dog sitting in a chair hunched over a winning stack of poker chips, green visor clamped firmly on his head, protecting his eyes from the bright lights. There was just one small flaw in his demeanor: Every time he was dealt a winning hand, he could not conceal his emotions as he would wag his tail.

Gestures. Psychology professors Paul Eckman and Wallace Friesen, both of the University of California Medical School, have identified several gestures that can get people in trouble, particularly business-people doing business in foreign countries:

- **The A-okay sign** *(thumb held to forefinger to make a ring)*. In the U.S. it means, "That's great" or "Right on." But in France and Belgium it means, "You're worth zero." In Greece and Turkey it is an invitation for sex or a vulgar insult.

- **The thumbs-up gesture.** In the U.S. it means, "Good," "All right" or "Ready to go." But in Greece, Sardinia, and in Arab countries it means, "Up yours."

- **Nodding the head up and down.** In the U.S. this gesture means "Yes, I agree" and generally is a sign of acceptance. Not so in Greece or Turkey, where it can mean "No" if the head is tilted high or if the nodding is accompanied by a clicking of the tongue.

- **Self-handshake** *(grabbing your own two hands and shaking them up and down) This is a form of self-applause to congratulate oneself* Prizefighters and politicians use this gesture to signify victory. Russians use this gesture to symbolize friendship or the desire to cooperate

So, when dealing with people of other backgrounds, take their gestures with a grain of salt as to what they might mean and go easy on your own gestures, lest you display your ignorance or inadvertently show a lack of respect.

The safest policy is to eliminate gestures unless you are certain of how they will be taken. As a matter of fact, even here in the U.S., with many people of different cultures, restraint is a virtue unless you are sure of the relationship.

Body language is a powerful sidekick that can reinforce the magic power of your words to communicate and influence others.

9 Barriers to Communication

It is important that you are understood,
but it is more important that you are not
misunderstood.

—Robert Louis Stevenson

Here is a story about what can go wrong if the communicator is not absolutely, positively clear about who is receiving the message:

> Running in a thick fog, the control center of a U.S. naval vessel suddenly spotted a blip on a radar screen. It appeared to be another vessel on a collision course with the U.S. ship. Seeing this, the captain radioed the message, "Alter your course immediately to 15 degrees starboard. This is a U.S. naval ship."
>
> The answer came back, "Alter *your* course 15 degrees starboard."
>
> When this message went to the bridge, the irate Navy captain's reply was, "Repeat. I strongly request you alter your course 15 degrees starboard immediately or I will blow you out of the water. ***This is the captain.***"
>
> Out of the fog came the answer, "Alter *your* course 15 degrees. ***This is the lighthouse!***"

Just think how much more effective our communications would be if everyone would wear a badge saying, "I know you think you understand what I just said, but I am not exactly sure you realize what you just heard is probably not what I meant."

The most powerful combination of words, yet the most difficult to say, are: "Before I answer you, my friend, I want to make sure that I understand what you mean." Learn to say this and you will improve your persuasive skills as a communicator 1000 percent. The key words to understanding are "ask" then "listen."

Your best moments as a communicator will be when you really try to *understand* someone's point of view, particularly if it differs from yours. You can control a conversation when you allow the other person to state his case, to take a stand, and let him state an opinion contrary to yours. Your most satisfying moment will be when you understand the other person's point of view. This is when you know you are in control.

There are just two basic rules for effective communications:

Rule 1. Put yourself in the mindset of the person to whom you are speaking.

Rule 2. Refer to rule one.

The major challenge to you as a communicator is: Do not assume that everyone else knows as much or is as intelligent as you. Never lose focus on the level of knowledge of the people you are talking to; these are the people who are listening to what you say. The question is, "Are these people hearing what you say? Are they hearing and understanding what you meant to convey?"

It is the job of the communicator to communicate; it is not the responsibility of the listener to understand what you meant to say. The meanings and perception of words are shaped by education, personal biases, assumptions, prejudices and the experiences of the people receiving your message.

An American and a British destroyer were on a joint mission. It was wartime, and the order was to travel in complete blackout. Plowing through the ocean at flank speed, the American ship saw a sliver of light piercing the blackness from the British ship. Pulling along the side the ship, the American captain signaled, "Put out your lights." Immediately the British ship was ablaze in light. After a salvo of "Put out your lights" messages back and forth, it dawned on the American captain that the British captain was following orders. He did *put out the lights*, more light and more light as he was ordered to do. So the American captain sent the message, "*Extinguish* your lights." Immediately the entire British ship was darkened. The words to *put out* and to *extinguish* meant different actions to different people.

Novelist Robert Louis Stevenson said, "In writing or speaking, it is important that you are understood, but it is more important that you are not misunderstood." When the person on the receiving end of a conversation misinterprets or does not comprehend what is being said, communication ends and conflict rears its ugly head.

Politicians and government agencies have the ability to take a simple issue and mutilate it beyond comprehension to the detriment of understanding. Here's how a government agency, the Bureau of Standards, responded to a perplexed plumber who wrote asking if it was safe to use hydrochloric acid to open clogged drainpipes. Here is the reply that came from a Bureau scientist:

> The uncertain reactive process of hydrochloric acid places the pipe in jeopardy when alkalinity is involved. The efficacy of this solution is indisputable, but the corrosive residue is incompatible with metallic permanence.

The perplexed plumber replied, thanking the Bureau for recommending his method. The scientist, after reading the thank you note, was disturbed by the misunderstanding. He shared the letter with his colleague who immediately wrote the plumber the following letter:

> Hydrochloric acid generates a toxic residue that will produce submuriate invalidating reactions. Some alternative procedure is preferable.

Once again the plumber, believing his procedure was acceptable, wrote back that he agreed with the Bureau and was glad to hear that, "Hydrochloric acid works just fine."

Greatly upset, the two scientists took their problem to their boss who asked his secretary to respond. The next day the plumber received a telegram from the secretary. It read: "Don't use hydrochloric acid. It eats the hell out of the pipes."

The scientists used a hundred multisyllabic words to say what twelve simple words said with great clarity. This is called "using the economy of words" to deliver your message with comprehension and understanding. The mark of a master communicator is to simplify the complicated. Too often people complicate the simple.

The objective of all verbal intercourse is to be heard, to be understood and to achieve the desired results. Plato summed it up neatly when he wrote, "Nothing is as important as saying the right thing in the right amount at the right time to the right people."

We have learned that the major barrier to satisfying interpersonal relations is to be understood and to achieve willing compliance. A leader cannot lead, a teacher cannot teach, a salesperson cannot sell unless they are understood. You are not leading unless you have followers. You are not teaching until someone learns. You are not selling until someone buys. Did you ever stop to wonder what would happen in all our relationships if we would give the other person equal billing? The switch might be from being a good teacher to being easy to learn from, from being a good salesman to being easy to buy from, from being a good parent to being easy to live with.

Being misunderstood is the prime barrier to effective communication. Other barriers that block the smooth transition of information follow.

- ***Lack of respect by either party for the other.*** It is a very human trait to dislike someone. When this occurs, communication stops, and the relationship becomes adversarial. It is your job as a communicator to short-circuit this situation. In all interpersonal relationships, the key to being a winner is in your perspective of how you see your adversary. When you look at someone whom you are trying to sell, inform, instruct, or inspire, do you see a recalcitrant, disagreeable, stubborn person who cannot be trusted and who is 180 degrees apart from your own personal opinions? Or, when you look at the other person, do you see an intelligent, trustworthy individual who is a fundamental resource to making you a winner?

  With the wrong perspective, no sale is made. Nobody wins.

But with the right perspective and mindset, leaders chalk-up a winning performance. This wins friends and influences people to like you and to buy from you, and makes you a winner. Put people first, brush aside petty annoyances and differences, and concentrate on being a winner.

Will Rogers once said, "I never met a man I didn't like." Look for the best in everyone you meet.

- *Failure to identify the purpose of the conversation.* All communication should have a purpose, a goal, and an objective to be accomplished. This is the rudder that steers the conversation on a straight course. A salesperson begins his presentation with, "I have an idea that will make you money and save you problems." A business manager says to an employee, "George, you are a valued employee with an enviable record of service, but one situation has developed that I would like to resolve to your satisfaction."

- *The communicator assumes the listener understands the message.* Imagine how much more effective we would be if we actually listened so we really understood, particularly those of us who make our living talking to people. It is important that you are understood, but it is more important that you are not misunderstood. Use the *broken mirror* tactic to assure that what you have just said is understood. Let's say you have just told someone you will meet him or her at 9:00 A.M. Monday morning for an important conference. To be certain they understand you, repeat the time and place, but make one mistake, saying, "Okay, I'll see you Monday at 10:00 A.M." If they correct you, then you know your message was understood. If no correction comes, you need to restate the time and place because you were misunderstood.

- *The communicator is not clear himself.* The communicator must be crystal clear as to the message to be conveyed. Otherwise, the conversation will lack direct relevance and wander aimlessly without direction or purpose.

- *Preconceptions of either party.* A preconception is a general thought or mental image that is solidly fixed in a mind that is closed to any new concepts. This is a mental barrier to the introduction of any new idea or concept. The communicator must be open-minded and able to find and identify these "set-in-concrete" conceptions in order to open the mind and control the conversation.

A human mind is like a parachute: It works best when it is open. There is one thing a successful communicator or salesperson must do: Change a listener's attitude from downright indifference or lukewarm attention into positive, favorable open-minded attention.

A tested and proven way to do this is to capture the listener's attention with the promise of a benefit so strong and personal that it arouses the desire to learn more:

> Joe, I have an idea that will guarantee you a substantial income for the rest of your life and you will never have to work another day.

- *Not open to feedback.* In every personal or business transaction there must be a *meeting of minds*. This takes the form of a mental agreement based upon mutual benefits and satisfaction. Without a responsive feedback of opinions and reaction, there is no conversation. Without a response, it is like whistling in the dark or delivering a sermon to an empty church. You know what you are saying, but no one is listening and there is no reaction.

  All conversation is related to action. The purpose of all dialogues is to reach a mutually beneficial conclusion or resolution compatible to both parties. When you are locked into a mute, no-response conversation, use *Force Communication Tactics* (a term popularized by Herschell Gordon Lewis) that demand a response. Ask questions, "What is your opinion?" "What do you believe?" Use imperative statements that command attention and use words that generate an emotional reaction.

  Use action verbs and adverbs that command action. Fred Smith, the founder of FedEx, had a passive slogan that said, "When it has to be there overnight." With the addition of two adverbs the slogan forced attention: "When it *absolutely positively* has to be there overnight." Words are charged with electric voltage.

• **Emotions are ignored.** Emotion is always in command over intellect. We do what our *feelers* (emotions) tell us to do, and then we call on our *thinkers* (intellectual logic) to justify our emotional decision. Emotions are the *hot buttons* that trigger all action.

The wrong words can create raw emotional reactions. The right words can soothe and refresh to put one in a positive, friendly frame of mind open to accepting information. People will retain and remember about 50 percent of what you tell them, but how you make them feel has a 100 percent retention rate. You win every time you make someone feel good about themselves.

• **Inertia.** It is easier for people to do nothing than to accept your proposition. Typical excuses that must be overcome include: I don't want to upset the status quo. I always do it my way. I like the way I am doing now; why change? I don't want to take a chance on something new.

To overcome inertia, you should anticipate questions in advance and answer them before they are asked. Have a strong value proposition and give a solid *Reason Why* it would be in their best interest to act now. Always clinch your argument by telling them *what they will lose if they don't act now.* Failure to get on the listener's level. Still true is the saying, "When in Rome, do as the Romans do." If you want to win an argument, make a sale or capture a mind, tailor your words to the same level of knowledge and your attire to match the environment of the person to whom you are talking. To match words and wits with wildcatters in the oil fields, wear a hardhat and use colloquial Anglo-Saxon English to communicate. If you are doing business in the ivory towers of corporate America, business dress is called for and you communicate with business verbiage.

• **Defenses are triggered.** Know in advance any prejudices, opinions, or fixations of the person to whom you are speaking. Nothing shatters a conversation faster than to trigger a negative reaction. Nothing shatters a conversation faster than to say, "I understand how you feel, *but.*" That one word, *but,* signals a disagreement and an ensuing argument. Winning communicators know better than to trigger defenses.

To summarize this chapter, I would like to point out that effective communicators are skillful controllers. They maneuver constantly, trying to figure out what is necessary to succeed and win the discussion, the argument, or the sale. Master communicators threaten when they have to and concede when they have to. They never lose sight of their objective, which is to win. But when they realize their objective cannot be accomplished, they arrange for a back door to escape with dignity and respect.

A top communicator needs to be an actor, a teacher, a strategist, an intimidator, and a confidant. Strangely enough, these skills are natural and instinctive. Everyone has them. Some people use them to create their own personal success; others fail to exercise them and never achieve fulfillment. Which are you?

Here are eight final tips that will make you a winner in dealing with people:

- Never censor people who entertain ideas and opinions different from yours, even though they might make you unhappy. Always remember, listening to and accepting differences of opinions is a sure path to enlightenment for you. Listen and act; do not react.
- The most important thing in getting others to talk is shutting up.
- The most important part of communications is listening.
- Learn to listen. Don't talk to fill the great void. Let others fill the void.
- Do not make any statement others know not to be true.
- Keep your ego in a jar. Only open it to stuff more knowledge in.
- To be trusted is more important than to be loved.
- Never pass the blame—it only makes you a loser. Accept the blame and you will always win.

10 It's Been Done Before

If you can dream it, you can do it.

—Walt Disney

Regardless of who you are or what you have been, you can be what you want to be.

—W. Clement Stone

Did you ever ask yourself these questions?

1. Who am I?
2. What am I known for?
3. Does anybody care?
4. How does this affect me?

Did you ever wonder why some people are successful and happy in their jobs and others fade into obscurity? The reason that some people are successful is because they are individuals with personal characteristics that make them stand out from the ordinary—they are known as a top sales person, an able administrator, a creative problem solver or a master communicator or . . . ? What are you known for?

What are your personal characteristics? How are you identified? What makes you unique or remarkable? What is your story? How would you tell it if you wanted to "Jump-Start" your career and your life?

I would suggest that the surest way to launch a new beginning would be to develop your skills and your strengths as a master communicator.

Wherever you go whatever your career choice you will be able to excel in persuading your boss, your colleagues and your subordinates about the wisdom of your ideas and the strength of your abilities.

Eight out of every ten people are not happy with their jobs. They don't like the people they work with. The boss doesn't appreciate them. They are not making enough money, and they have a burning desire for a job that is more fulfilling, enjoyable, and financially rewarding.

Do you ever ask yourself, "What am I doing in this job? I don't enjoy what I'm doing. I really should get out of here, but I'm scared to take a chance."

If these thoughts have crossed your mind, it is never too late to make a change in your life. Regardless of what you are or what you have been, you can be what you want to be. Now is the time to *jump-start your life* and convert your dreams for financial success and happiness into reality.

Stop for a minute and listen to yourself. What would you really like to do? If you could do anything you wanted to do, what would it be? How would you finish this sentence, "Someday I would like to. . . . "? What is the goal of your life? Psychologists have a devilishly effective way of ferreting out the truth. They would ask you to write your own obituary. How would you like it to read? How would you like to be remembered? Do this and be truthful. This is your real goal in life. Refer to it and read it every day. One more thing: Share this with a friend. This way you commit yourself to be all you want to be.

I encouraged a friend of mine to take this test. At forty years of age he was shackled to a routine, no-win job. He admitted he would like to make a change, but lacked the courage to face the problem directly. I asked him to write his obituary as to how he would like to be remembered, which he did reluctantly. Here's the essence of what he wrote, "I would like to be remembered as a man who had many friends who looked to me for support and counsel whenever they needed a helping hand or a lift up. I would like to have a job that involved a close association with people, a job I would love so much that I could not wait to go to work every day." I reminded Mike that if he ever found a job like this, he would never have to work another day in his life.

After reading his "obit" I said, "Mike, you just wrote a job description for a career in selling." Mike looked me square in the eye and replied, "Sales! Not for me. I couldn't take the rejections and insults.

Besides, I don't believe I have the courage to call on people I don't know and ask them to buy from me." I parried this remark with, "Mike, you're looking at sales through the wrong end of the telescope. Selling is not aggression. Salespeople are *purchase advisors* who help friends and customers make wise buying decisions. People in sales help their customers solve problems. That's all there is to sales: bringing good products to people so they can live a happier and trouble-free life." Then I added the clincher, saying, "Mike, you've got more guts and courage than you give yourself credit for. Use it now or lose it."

Mike reluctantly took my advice and found a job as a sales assistant. He soon discovered that interfacing with people and helping them make wise buying decisions was not only financially rewarding, but fun, too. He thanked me for encouraging him to find this niche for himself. Then he added the clincher; he told me, "Bob, I don't worry anymore about getting a paycheck. In sales, I write my own paychecks, and I like it this way."

Here's another story of a man you know. He failed a few times but never gave up his desire for success. He failed two times in business then decided to run for the state legislature. He ran and lost. Back into business he went and failed again. Back into politics again. He ran and was elected to the state legislature. Moving up, he ran for Speaker of the House, but was defeated.

Determined and filled with desire, he ran for Congress and was elected, but was defeated for a second term. Undaunted, he ran for the U.S. Senate and lost two times. He even lost a bid for Vice President of the United States.

This man was a loser, but his desire and expectations continued on a high level. Two years after his last defeat he ran for President of the United States. This time he made it. You know his name: Abraham Lincoln.

This is proof that it is never too late, and you are never too old to start over.

Age doesn't matter. Abraham Lincoln and Henry Ford were past their primes when success came into their lives. Ben Franklin was just sixteen when he published his first newspaper, and he helped frame the U.S. Constitution at the age of eighty-one.

Have you ever asked yourself, am I really doing what I would like to do? What can I do to make more money and enjoy what I'm doing?

How often have you looked at people you know who have money and are successful and wondered what they did to make money? Then you posed the question, "What do they have that makes them so successful? They enjoy perks and privileges, travel first class, and dress like James Bond." Then the thought runs through your mind: "I'm smarter than they are. Why can't I get a job that makes me successful and rich?" The answer is: "You can!" Regardless of who you are or what you have been, you can be whatever you desire to be. Just set your goal and don't give up.

Now I am asking you, "What is holding you back?"

If your answer is "self confidence," you are not alone. In a recent survey conducted by a national research firm, people were asked, "What is our most difficult personal problem?" Eighty-five percent of those surveyed answered, "Self confidence."

If you are asking yourself these questions, maybe it is time to take control and jump-start your life. You do have a choice. If you are satisfied and happy with what you are doing and have achieved all you ever wanted, that's okay. Enjoy. But if you want to better your position in life and take control of your life, put your desires in writing. Write it down! Today!

All personal achievement starts in the mind of the individual. You know exactly what you desire, what you dream to have in your life. Only you know your problem. You are the only one who knows the goal you want to achieve in your life.

The most important sale you will ever make is that of selling yourself on taking control of your life. Once you are in control of your life, set goals and a timetable for accomplishing them. Then, commit your goals to writing. Write it down.

When you put your dreams in black and white, you will have taken the first step to making good things happen in your life. Tell everyone what you want to do and someone will step in to help you. Every day check up on yourself, refer to what you have written and ask yourself, "Am I on track for achieving my desires?" If you are not meeting the requirements you have set for yourself, immediately take corrective action and pull yourself back on track. It is important that you plan your goals and pursue them with determination and gusto. If you don't do this, your dreams will fade into pipe dreams.

Here's the story of a man named Angelo Siciliano, a youngster who even as a young boy had a dream and a goal of becoming the world's best developed man. Angelo had standards toward which he was working. He wanted to develop a 50-inch chest, 17-inch biceps and a 17½-inch neck. Every week he would measure himself, comparing each week's measurements with the previous week.

Over the years he became a physical specimen. He was no longer a skinny, scrawny little boy. He was a wonderfully developed man, and the name "Angelo" had turned to the nickname "Charlie." One evening a New York City policeman named "Butch," with muscles to match his name, was watching Charlie lift weights. As he added more and more weight, Butch asked Charlie, "What are you trying to do, become Atlas?" (In Greek mythology Atlas was a Titan who was compelled to hold the heavens on his shoulders.) This was precisely what Charlie was trying to do, so he adopted the name: Charles Atlas.

A man named Bernard MacFadden, publisher of a New York newspaper and a promoter, ran a contest to find the world's most handsome man. The event was held at New York's Madison Square Garden. "Muscle Men" gathered from around the world to compete for the title and the prizes.

Charles Atlas won and for many subsequent years stood in the winner's circle.

From this accomplishment Charlie launched a body-building business that in turn developed into a very successful comic strip. The comic strip featured a skinny man, in the company of a well-endowed lady, at the beach having sand kicked into his face by a muscle-bound bully. To avenge this embarrassment, the next frame showed the skinny Mr. Milquetoast attending a Charles Atlas dynamic tension class. Then, you guessed it, the next scene showed the reconstructed man, muscles bulging, giving the bully a taste of his new strength and courage—of course, to the loving delight of the young lady.

This new body-building business made Charles Atlas world famous and his marvelous body known and admired by millions of fans.

Charlie lived a long and prosperous life. He became a family man and a grandfather respected by all who knew him. Throughout his entire life he maintained the body that had won him so many accolades and awards.

There were many times when Charlie felt like quitting, but he persevered. He hung in there and stuck with this goal. This story of

Charles Atlas is the formula of success for you. Here is the seven-point plan that can make you successful:

1. Decide what you want to accomplish.
2. Paint this picture vividly in your mind.
3. Write in black and white exactly what you want to accomplish.
4. Execute your plan and "fake" what you want to be until you "make it."
5. Check-up on yourself to see if you are on target.
6. Challenge yourself to keep a positive mental attitude.
7. Don't give up. Stick with it.

Set your goal and stick with it. Think positive thoughts. Do this with determination and resolve, and your success is an absolute certainty. You'll be able to look at yourself in the mirror and say with authority and conviction, "*I am a happy and successful human being. I have friends and the power to favorably influence people.*" You will be right, too, because you will have made it so.

The cornerstone of being successful in everything you do is to *maintain a positive mental attitude.* Be optimistic. Think positive thoughts. Even if life throws you a curve, keep your head and only think positive thoughts; even in adversity there lay the seeds of success.

Thomas Edison is a classic example of the power of positive thinking. Edison failed hundreds of times when trying to discover the right filament for his incandescent light. When asked about his failures he replied, "I discovered many hundreds of things that would not work before I discovered the right filament."

Edison was an inquisitive man. He was always probing to find the right answer to problems. If he could not get the right answer, he would dig deeper and ask the simple question: Why? Edison was a thinker, too. On his desk was a quote by the portrait painter, Sir Joshua Reynolds, "There is no expedient to which a man will not resort to avoid the real labor of thinking."

"Think and Grow Rich" is a phrase that should be imbedded in the mind of anyone who wants to better their position in life. *Think and Grow Rich* is also the title of an inspirational book written by Napoleon Hill. The book is filled with stories of how men and women raised themselves from failure to success through the magic of positive thinking. Hill devoted his life to interviewing successful men and women and then revealing their secrets for success in the pages of his book.

W. Clement Stone was a cohort of Napoleon Hill. As a young man of nineteen, he started selling insurance. His tenacity and optimism propelled him into a multimillion-dollar insurance enterprise. He developed a lifelong philosophy of the power of a positive mental attitude. He shared this belief in three books, *A Success System That Never Fails*, *The Other Side of the Mind*, and *Success through a Positive Mental Attitude*, which he coauthored with Napoleon Hill. Both men were extremely successful and wealthy beyond their imaginations.

Some of Hill's inspirational quotations still ring true today:

Whatever the mind can conceive and believe, it can achieve.

Success comes to those who are success conscious.

Desire is the starting point of all achievement.

Anybody can wish for riches, and most people do, but only a few know a definite plan, plus a burning desire for wealth, is the only dependable means of accumulating wealth.

Some of Stone's quotations include:

Aim for the moon. If you miss, you may hit a star.

Be careful of the environment you choose for it will shape you: be careful of the friends you choose for you will become like them.

A definite purpose is the starting point for all achievement.

Success is achieved and maintained by those who try and keep trying.

Try, try, try and keep on trying is the rule that must be followed to become an expert in anything.

When you discover your mission, you will feel its demand. It will fill you with enthusiasm and a burning desire to get to work on it.

W. Clement Stone was like a character right from the pages of a Horatio Alger novel. During the last quarter of the nineteenth century, Horatio Alger wrote inspirational stories about boys who were raised in poverty but through their own tenacity and desire to be successful, made good in life. Stone was a classic example of this, and to honor his rise from a humble beginning to riches, he was inducted into the Horatio Alger Association of Distinguished Americans.

Stone was firm in his belief that people remember the unusual. He personified this in his dress and flamboyant appearance. He always presented a very striking appearance with his brightly colored suspenders, polka-dot bow ties, and his pencil-thin mustache, all accented with spats on his shoes. He was always meticulously dressed in the latest of fashion.

His striking outward appearance was equally matched by his ability as a communicator and salesman. He believed in his power to be successful, and his most quoted remark was, "All I want to do is change the world." He did, too. The money he made in the business world he shared generously with others. Throughout his life, W. Clement Stone donated over $275 million dollars to charitable organizations, including the Boys and Girls Clubs of America, youth development, education, and self-improvement projects to help young people break free of their environment and achieve success in their lives. Mr. Stone had a solid conviction that every individual should make a significant contribution to improving the quality of life for others.

W. Clement Stone's goal was not to be famous. He just wanted to lift himself out of the rubble of Chicago's west side. In the process, he discovered the power of a "Positive Mental Attitude." Coupled to this, he believed in the power of optimism and that even in adversity lay the seeds of success. Stone was a master communicator, a master persuader who became wealthy and famous for doing something great and meaningful.

Another man whose career paralleled the arc of W. Clement Stone's life was Babe Herman. But his career wasn't in business; it was in sports. He was hitting home runs and becoming a legend while Stone was building an insurance empire. Herman was one of the most noted power hitters in the 1930s. He gained fame and recognition while playing right field for the Brooklyn Dodgers. His career slugging average at that time was .532, which means that more than 50 percent of his hits were extra base hits. When he retired in 1945, his .393 batting average, .678 slugging average, 241 hits, and 416 total bases were and still remain a Dodgers franchise record.

Obviously, Herman was an outstanding hitter, but he was renowned for his goofs as a defensive player and base runner. This earned him boos and catcalls from the Brooklyn fans.

His fielding frailties were comedies of errors. At right field, fly balls fell through his hands and grounders snaked through his legs. A newspaper sports writer once wrote, "Babe Herman only wears a glove because it's part of the uniform." Another fielding error that added to his fame: Babe was on second base when a teammate hit a home run. Babe was so excited he stopped to watch the ball fly over the fence. The home run hitter ran the bases while Babe, stopped at second base, was still gawking. The result, what should have been two runs counted only as one.

The Brooklyn Bleacher Bums were noted for violent reactions to errors, and any player who made an error was roundly and soundly booed. Babe Herman was the exception. His Brooklyn fans loved him for his booming bat and forgave his fielding frailties.

One day while playing right field, a sizzling grounder zipped right between the Babe's legs and under his outstretched glove. There was stunned silence from the Brooklyn bleachers. There was not a boo or a catcall, just silence. Babe was mad and obviously agitated with his fielding error. Babe *spit* into his glove and, with obvious anger, pounded his fist into his glove several times. Finally a fan jumped up to break the stunned silence and hollered down to the disgusted Babe, "Nice spit, Babe!" The entire stadium erupted in laughter. To make up for his error, Babe went on to hit three home runs in the game.

The chronicles of business, the professions, sports, science, and the arts are filled with the accomplishments of women who leveraged their strengths and unique talents to success. A classic example is Mary Kay Ash, who founded Mary Kay Cosmetics and is recognized as one of America's greatest female entrepreneurs.

Mary Kay Cosmetics began with a dream, a dream to build a company where women could achieve unlimited success. In 1963 Mary Kay retired from a very successful career in direct sales with Stanley Home Products. She retired because a man whom she had trained was promoted over her. Mary Kay vowed that in her direct sales company, Mary Kay Cosmetics, women would be given every opportunity to excel;

and sales excellence was rewarded. Top sales performers were awarded pink Cadillac's, which became an icon for Mary Kay Cosmetics.

Mary Kay wrote three best selling books, the last one entitled *You Can Have It All.* Her sales philosophy is included in the business course at Harvard University

Not content with the 2.2 billion dollars in worldwide sales that Mary Kay Cosmetics' sales consultants have generated and her international reputation as a successful business woman, she initiated a Mary Kay Ash Charitable Foundation for cancer and domestic violence.

Cynthia Kersey, author of *Unstoppable,* reveals the secret of becoming "unstoppable." She spent years researching and interviewing many of America's greatest achievers and outlines an easy-to-follow plan that anyone can apply to create unstoppable results in their lives.

Cynthia's personal story is the basis for her book and her message. She started life as a secretary, and then rose to the position of sales executive at Sprint Communications.

Throughout her journey she has been a Master Communicator pursuing her dreams and sharing her principle of being unstoppable with others through her writing and seminars. She has appeared on television with Oprah Winfrey and presented seminars to a host of Fortune 500 companies. Her message empowers people to create a rich and meaningful life.

Every man and every woman is a unique individual. Everyone has a unique point of difference. No two people are alike. Each has his or her unique style. Many attributes combine to make up an individual. When used to advantage they have a powerful impact on the ability to achieve success, happiness and money.

Some of the factors that impact success are:

- Moral characteristics
- Education and knowledge
- Experiences
- Innate talent and skills
- Physical characteristics
- Language and communication skills
- Self-perception
- Desire

The anchor of all these attributes—and the one that is the catalyst that propels you to success—is *desire*. You must have a burning desire to achieve fame and fortune.

The world is filled with well-educated and trained men and women who never reach their full potential because their desire is lost in dreams, not action. *Desire* is an action word that must be coupled with determination and persistence. When you know what you desire to accomplish in your life, commit yourself to it and do not deviate from your course. Set your mental compass and let nothing cause you to stray from your desired goal.

I had a client whose name was Ross Wright. Ross was a super sales-man. He took great pride in being able to convince and persuade prospects to buy. Whenever someone stopped by his automobile show-room, Ross was challenged to make a sale.

One morning I dropped by his office for coffee. Ross was visibly shaken and out of sorts. I inquired, "Ross, what's the problem?" With a disgusted shake of his head he said, "Bob, yesterday, a man stopped in to look at a new car. I knew he wanted to own it and I pulled every clincher in the book to get him to sign the contract and take delivery of his new car. He wouldn't budge. Finally I said to him, "If you desire to own this car badly enough, you will find some way to get it.

"Would you believe me if I told you that he came back last night and stole the car?"

I tried to soothe his shattered ego telling him, "Ross that just goes to prove you are a master sales communicator. You created the desire to have that car, and you got action."

Another man with desire to succeed was Julius Caesar. Born with unbridled ambition and unsurpassed oratory skills, Caesar had a burn-ing desire to conquer Pompei, the ruler of Rome. An ancient Roman law forbade any general from crossing the Rubicon River and entering Italy proper with an army.

To do so was treason. This tiny stream, called the Rubicon, was Caesar's point of no return.

Aware of the consequences, Julius Caesar massed his legions along the Rubicon, knowing full well that once he crossed it, he was commit-ted. The only reward was victory. To be defeated was total annihilation and death. Caesar didn't hesitate. As he crossed the river to realize his desire for victory over Pompei and the conquest of Rome, Caesar cried out, "Let us go where our gods and our enemies summon us! The die is cast."

This is a perfect example of desire, dedication and commitment; this is the not-so secret secret of what it takes to win success and fortune. We all know this, but few practice it. Admiral David Farragut, hero of New Orleans and Mobile Bay during the Civil War, uttered this historic challenge as his ship met the Confederate blockade, "Damn the torpedoes, full speed ahead." Nothing would stop him from his appointed mission to win.

With men and women who have dreams of their personal conquest for fame and fortune, their obstacle often is indecision, fear of making a mistake, fear of ridicule, fear of failure. How about you? If you're not happy with where and what you are and desire a change, do you have the courage to start all over again—to damn the torpedoes or to cross your Rubicon?

It's never too late or never too early to do what you want to do or to be what you want to be. There is no time limit. Start whenever you are ready to commit. It's your call, change or stay in the rut you are in. What do you desire?

Regardless of who you are or what you have been, you can be what you want to be. Your first and most important step is to *sell* and convince yourself that you desire to make a change for the better in your life. Selling yourself will be the toughest challenge you will have to face. The rest is easy. Then you are on your way to managing your life and this can lead you to fame and fortune.

Winston S. Churchill in an address to the boys of Harrow School in England reminded the boys to never give in with these words:

Never give in, never give in
Never, never, never, never—
In nothing great or small
Large or petty—
Never give in
Except to convictions of honor
And good sense!

11 Wanted: People Who Want to Earn Money and Have Fun, Too

People are always blaming their circumstances for what they are. I don't believe in circumstances. The people who get on in this world are the people who get up and look for the circumstances they want, and if they can't find them, they make them.

—George Bernard Shaw

Paul Harvey, noted radio commentator and considered by many to be the greatest salesman in the history of radio, commented many times about salesmanship. I remember one of his remarks started with "Wanted: Salespersons," "The rest of the Story . . . " (Harvey's trademark)continues: Help wanted Salespersons. Now how can you explain eight percent unemployment when the daily paper includes all those help-wanted ads for anybody willing to get off his dead center and start selling something?

Is it because we have bred and schooled a batch of stick-in-the-mud malcontents who lack the guts, gumption and the get-up-and-go that we had a generation ago?

And if so, how can they get their get-up-and-go back?

Our nation's comparatively few prominent positive thinkers are trying with books, blandishments, seminars and correspondence courses to build a bonfire of ambition under this sleepy-eyed generation.

Yet the ads are still there—Help Wanted Salespersons.

And those millions who aren't working are still living off the efforts of the rest of us.

If somewhere down the road ahead our magnificent republic, which cost so many so much, drowns in red ink it will go down screaming: 'Help Wanted: Sales.'

In the first chapter of this book, I made the statement that all goods and services are a liability until they are moved. It costs money to manufacture, to store, to ship, to distribute. Nothing happens until somebody buys something, and nobody buys anything until they are convinced the benefits they will enjoy are worth more than the money it will cost them. In other words, until they've been sold. This is basic Economics 101 that defines the manufacturing of goods, their distribution, and their final consumption. At every turn on the highway of industry and commerce there is a sales communicator bringing the buyer and the seller together to the mutual benefit of the parties to the transaction.

People will always need goods and services, and there will always be a need for sales communicators to guide, help, and advise consumers on making a wise and practical decision. A sales communicator's very privileged job is to be a helpful *Purchase Advisor*. This is a man or a woman who has the ability to communicate wise and helpful information.

The quickest way to get what you want is to help someone else get what he or she wants. The Romans had a phrase for this: *quid pro quo*; literally, this for that. You do something good for me, and I will return the favor. You sell me a product that solves a problem for me, and I will give you money in return. That way we both profit.

At this point you might say, "Selling is not for me. I don't want to haggle and argue and be insulted by people." I have a very wealthy friend who made his fortune as a salesman. He wanted his son to follow in his footsteps and carve a career for himself in sales. He talked his son into becoming a salesman. After a few months on the sales firing line, the boy confided in his father, saying, "Dad, selling is not for me." The father asked, "Why?" His son explained, "I like being my own boss, and I do enjoy the commissions I am paid for my efforts and the fact I control my destiny and write my own pay check; but, Dad, I just cannot take the verbal insults."

Dad gave this remark a moment to set in and told the boy, "Son, I've been in sales for thirty years. I have had doors slammed in my face, telephones hung up on me, and been cursed at a few times, too. But in all my years I have never been insulted. Any bad experience I ever had was overshadowed by the friends I made along the way and the fortune I acquired."

Then Dad added his final piece of advice, saying, "Son, the fault is yours. It is your job as a communicator to stay on top of the sales conversation. You're probably talking too much! Your job is to control the conversation. To do this, ask questions and listen.

"You see, when people are talking about themselves and expressing their wishes and desires, they don't have time to think about you. They are concentrating on themselves and sharing their thoughts and desires with you. You are in complete control when you ask questions and listen—you are learning and you are in control, too.

"The ability to communicate and persuade others to your point of view is not a God-given talent; it is a skill that must be learned, nurtured, and practiced. As in any profession or craft, it takes time to become skilled and proficient as a master sales communicator."

Like it or not, whoever you are, whatever you do, you are practicing salesmanship every day of your life. You are selling something to someone. It may only be your opinion or point of view (as opposed to, say, a nuclear power plant), but you are practicing the art of persuasion. Similarly, every day someone is selling you something. Every day you are buying and every day you are selling. When you buy products or services, you are being sold on the benefits you will enjoy in return for the money you spend. When you decide not to buy you are selling, too, giving the salesperson all the reasons why you don't want to buy.

How many times in your life have you listened to someone trying to persuade you to exchange your money for a product or service and thought to yourself, "What a lousy sales job" or "What a tacky presentation"? And then the thought crossed your mind, "I could do a better job myself."

If you answered *yes* to this question, you are on your way to becoming a Master Communicator. Matter of fact, if you recognize a shabby sales talk and claim that you could do it better, you are taking a giant step to a new and rewarding career for yourself. If you are one who always looks for a better deal and willingly negotiates the transaction in your favor, you are highly qualified for a career in sales. If you answered *yes* to all of these questions, run—don't walk—to answer the first advertisement reading, "Wanted, Salespeople." You will have taken the first step to a successful, enjoyable and profitable career.

In the 1930s, at the apex of the Great Depression, men and women without a wage-earning job, desperate to earn money, took jobs as salespeople. Whenever a company hung out a sign that read, "Sales job available," the lines extended blocks long. Few were hired, but those who were and dedicated themselves to becoming master sales persuaders earned top commissions and sailed unscathed through those difficult years.

Two such men parlayed their sales skills into sales and marketing dynasties: Charles Kettering, the president of General Motors at the height of the worst Depression year, 1933, and Thomas Watson, CEO of IBM. Both of these men learned their sales skills under the disciplined tutelage of John Patterson, founder of National Cash Register Company—today known as NCR.

While president of GM, Kettering said, "You can't sell anything to anybody if he is perfectly happy with what he has." Then he went on to say, "I believe business will come back when you get some products that people want to buy. I am not worried about the future of America. I am only worried about how long we are going to wait for business to come back instead of going out and finding it and bringing it back. You've got to coax it back. It isn't going to come back by itself."

General Motors and IBM had great and innovative products, but the engine that provided the power to sell and move people to buy was American salesmanship.

It is interesting to note that, three-quarters of a century later, the United States of America is in the midst of another economic crisis. We are on the frightening fringe of a recession that could lead to another depression of massive proportions. That is, of course, unless corrective action is taken to restore faith and confidence in the economy.

The United States of America is poised at the dawn of a new era of progress and leadership. The challenges and the opportunities are in the major areas of geopolitics, culture, military, technology, and demography. This new era of world leadership cries for men and women who are master communicators.

Ralph Waldo Emerson built a protective barrier around this debilitating thought when he wrote, "Do the thing you fear, and the death of fear is certain." Your desire for success must be greater than your fear of failure.

It is interesting to note that in the year 2009 General Motors was on the verge of bankruptcy and had slipped to number two in the world automotive market. This disaster may just be the catalyst that will generate new and innovative GM products in the market. GM management should revive the principles of innovation and salesmanship espoused by Charles Kettering to lift them out of the cellar and into prominence once again. It has been done before, and it can be done again.

Great new products, great new services, and the development of super-interesting things will restore confidence and prosperity. The engine that will make good things happen is a return to the principles of salesmanship that moves people to buy products and services. Nothing happens until somebody sells something.

The only recession-proof, depression-proof skill I know is salesmanship. When you are recognized as a master communicator in your field, you will have reached the top of your profession. You will be your own boss, you will write your own paycheck. When you generate profitable sales, you are the vital and essential cog in the business. Finance and production are important, but nothing happens until somebody sells something. I'm not saying that sales is the only thing that makes a business profitable, but it is way ahead of whatever is second. Salesmanship is the power that persuades people to purchase products that others produce.

When asked what he considered to be the most important function in business—finance, production, or selling—Andrew Carnegie answered with another question: "What is the most important leg of a three-legged stool?" Consider the three legs as:

- Finance (investment capital)
- Production (the manufacturing process)
- Selling (distribution and consumption)

They are all vital. Take any one away, and it renders the other two useless. Management has learned that profits are only made when people purchase the goods factories produce . . . after salespeople bring in the orders.

According to a report by the U.S. Department of Commerce, United States industries do not usually have serious problems with financing or production. The primary problem is distribution; that is, the sale and movement of goods from manufacturers to jobbers, to wholesalers, to dealers, and retail outlets. Every movement of goods through the channels of distribution requires the articulate communication and professional service of a salesperson. Nothing happens until somebody sells something.

This is true for all products, but especially so for new products. New products, especially innovative ones, do not sell themselves. People are generally apprehensive about accepting the new and different. They have a tendency to hang onto the old and familiar. It takes time to be sold and convinced of the benefits and advantages that new and unusual products and services will bring. New ideas need a "seasoning" time before people will accept them. Few are courageous enough to step up and be the first to experience the new and untried.

Men and women who dream up new ideas and innovations know in advance that they face pessimism and inertia. Advertising, promotion, publicity, public relations, and intense communications are essential to opening the consumer's mind to accept the new, the unusual, and the different. There is a saying, "At every turn on the road to the future someone is posted to guard the past."

Few if any new discoveries are an immediate success. It takes time for new ideas and innovations to penetrate the consciousness of the human mind. This is even true in breakthrough medical technology that promises users better health, discoveries that promise to improve the quality of life, and scientific discoveries that open new horizons into the mysteries of our minds and the world in which we live.

It is a human frailty that prompts people to be wary of the new and unproven, and to say, "It sounds like a great idea, but you go first. I'll try it later." The development of any new product or innovation that is introduced to the public is super-risky. The cycle from production to consumption has a soft spot in the middle called marketing and distribution; good things don't happen until somebody sells something. You must move people to buy to move merchandise off the shelves or out of the storeroom—only when this happens is profit generated.

The last few years of the nineteenth century and the beginning of the twentieth century saw the introduction of many innovative products that, if accepted, would have immediately altered the course of business. This was not the case; the benefits lay dormant in the minds of consumers until salespeople, convinced of the value of their products, opened the minds and the pocketbooks of wary consumers.

Six of the trendsetting discoveries that were not immediately accepted were: Elecricity, the typewriter, the telephone, the radiotelegraph system, the accounting machine called the cash register, and the automobile. Today, you rely on updated variations of these products, to run your home and your business efficiently. Not so when they were first introduced. Until late in the nineteenth century electricity was a scientific curiosity. People were afraid to use it for fear of fire. The typewriter was not immediately accepted. Office workers viewed it as complicated, and they didn't want to learn a new skill. Management rejected it because a letter written in formal type looked too impersonal. Christopher Sholes pioneered the development of the typewriter, but for financial reasons he was forced to sell his patent to the Remington Arms Company. They manufactured weapons, but they had the vision to see the value to business of this new contraption called a typewriter—a Remington typewriter.

It took a century before a new idea and innovation called the computer and the Internet antiquated the typewriter.

Alexander Graham Bell introduced the telephone as a business tool, but management scoffed at the idea of using an electric toy in the operation of their business. Managers were happy with the status quo; Why would they need to use a telephone? All business was personal and face-to-face; the telephone was too impersonal. Bell had so many financial setbacks that at one point he offered to sell the entire project to Western Union. Much to his dismay at the time, the president of the Western Union rejected the offer. He lacked the vision to see the innovation of the future. Today we have the multipurpose cell phone—the telephone that serves as a camera, takes motion pictures, and serves as a road map and navigation device plus, it serves as a computer to receive and send messages.

Guglielmo Marconi discovered the radiotelegraph system of wireless telegraphy. People complained that his wireless system was causing disruptive interference with their present system. He was plagued with lawsuits and patent infringements. He asked one time, "Have I done the world good or is it a nuisance?" Yet ultimately he prevailed.

As I pointed out previously, the National Cash Register Company was the brainchild of John Patterson. He was a proud and arrogant man with an ego to match. His life had been in retail sales. When he was away from the store, he noticed money and profit disappeared. He discovered that employees were putting money in their pockets instead of the cash drawer.

At about this same time Patterson became aware of a company manufacturing cash registers, a machine designed to stifle internal theft. He bought the company and changed its name to National Cash Register Company. Sales were not easy. Business was satisfied with the old system of accounting: All monies were secured in a locked drawer and records were maintained with pen and ink handwriting.

Patterson understood the problem of internal pilferage. He was convinced his product was the solution to the problem, but business management was not ready to accept this innovation because it had not been proven successful. Today the cash register has been replaced with computerized accounting machines.

Henry Ford gave us the Model T (the "Tin-Lizzy"). The first Fords were developed and sold to the well-to-do who could afford the $995 sales price. But through his genius for mass production and assembly-line efficiency, the sales price was eventually lowered to $295, and the automobile became an essential form of transportation for the ordinary citizen.

Henry Ford did not have an easy time convincing the American public that his "horseless carriage" was the new way of transportation. Die-hards who believed horsepower had four legs dug in their heels (or hooves) and refused to accept this noisy chugging piece of metal that caused their horses to bolt and become unruly.

Henry Ford was once asked in an interview if he did research to determine whether or not the public wanted his horseless carriage. Ford replied, "No, absolutely not. It is not possible for people to respond intelligently to something about which they know nothing. Most people see things only in relation to that with which they are familiar." Then he added, "If I were to ask someone who has always used a horse for transportation, what would you like to have to speed-up your travel?" Ford answered his own question with, "Most people are not familiar with the horseless carriage but well aware of the benefit of a horse would probably answer 'a faster horse.'"

People generally don't know what they specifically want. Only when a new idea or innovation is introduced to them do they allow their mind to open and consider the benefits. A persuader/salesman/master communicator is the catalyst that brings new ideas into focus. Nothing happens until somebody sells something.

The quality of salesmanship today leaves much to be desired. A very high proportion of those engaged in selling cannot sell; they lack the ability, the attitude, and the training. Plus, they are not willing to learn and practice the principles that will make them good communicators.

Enormous amounts of manpower and money are wasted today because management doesn't really know what selling is about, nor do they understand how its effectiveness can be enhanced. Too many businesses are flawed by lawyers and financial geniuses who are skilled at manipulating money but don't know how to motivate people. Perhaps the time has come for the boardrooms of businesses to be taken over by communication and marketing professionals.

More importantly, men and women in the work force do not understand the rewards a career in selling can bring. Selling is viewed as a menial job, only a temporary expedient until a position commensurate with "my" personal talents can be found. This is not true. Today, there is a completely new environment. Supply of goods has outstripped demand. Thanks to the Internet, customers have more information and more choices about what, where, and how they can acquire goods and services.

Today, customers are demanding more from their suppliers. As the sales environment becomes more challenging, career sales professionals are learning to create more value in every sale. Competition that doesn't match this value-added service will be left in the sales dust.

I am currently in the process of buying a new automobile. Uncertain of the make and model I wanted, I explored the showrooms of the three top American car dealerships plus the European and Asian competition. What I discovered was a complete lack of product knowledge and an appalling lack of communication skill. Only one salesperson out of seven dealerships visited bothered to get my name and call me back. Not a single one bothered to find out what model I wanted. All greeted me with, "We'll give you best deal in town." Not a single salesperson (and I use the word loosely) bothered to communicate the *value* to me of the convenience, service and personal attention I would receive at their place of business.

At another stop I walked past what looked like three sales types. As I passed by them, not one bothered to greet me. I walked to the lady receptionist and said, "I am interested in buying a car. Is there someone here who could help me?" Hearing this, one of the sales types sauntered over, hands in his pockets, and said, "Maybe I can help you. What are you looking for?" My silent thought was, "A new car, Stupid. This is an automobile showroom, isn't it?"

At another dealer showroom, the "salespeople" were a little more aggressive. I was looking at a model that caught my eye. A sales type saw me and said, "We've got a special deal going today. It's the end of the month, and we have to move cars." I countered with, "How much? What's the price?" With this, I was ushered into a cubicle and offered, "coffee, Coke, or water?" Then, out of nowhere, another person was introduced as the sales manager. This guy was a trained "closer," and his first question was, "We're ready to deal. What do I have to do to get you to buy this car today?" Before I could answer he was at me again with what sales trainers refer to as the "assumptive close," asking, "If we make the deal this afternoon, which color would you prefer, red or grey?" Between the salesman and the manager I felt like a ping-pong ball being pummeled from two sides.

In desperation, I stood and said, "Listen, gentlemen, I'm serious about buying a car. Mine comes off lease next month, and I want to replace it with, hopefully, an American-made car. I just want to know your lowest price and why it would be to my advantage to buy from you." Then I gave the two of them another lead, saying, "I live in this town, and I want the convenience of a service department."

I got an answer, but not the right one. I was told, "Mr. Hemmings, when you are ready to buy, bring us your best deal and we will beat it." I gave them my business card but have not had one phone call or follow-up.

Finally, I found the right car at the right price and the right monthly payment terms. I was happy and told the salesman with whom I made the deal to get the papers ready for me to sign. After a half-an-hour wait and a cup of coffee, the papers were presented for me to sign. I was informed by the salesman he had made a very small glitch and the payment was just a few more bucks a month, ten dollars to be exact. I thought to myself, "Ten dollars a month times thirty-six months, that's $360 right to the dealer's bottom line and that spells extra profit." With this, another thought raced through my mind, "Whatever happened to integrity and honesty?" I ripped the contract into pieces, said, "No thanks," and walked out. As I was getting into my car, the salesman ran to me, saying breathlessly, "My manager told me you can forget the extra ten dollars." As I drove out, he was still standing there mumbling to himself.

After much searching, I finally found the car I wanted. It was the right color, had the right accessories, was available at a dealer close to my home and I knew from my research online that it was the right price. This was all accomplished without the interference or interruption of any sales help. Now I wanted to negotiate the sale and I needed an order taker.

At the dealership I saw a man leaning against a car and asked if he was a salesman. He responded with, "Yes, can I help you?" He should have asked "May I help you?" but I wasn't one to correct the grammar of a car salesman. To his offer to help I said, "Yes." Touching the car, I added, "I want to buy this car."

After being ushered into the sales manager's office and the usual offer of a Coke, coffee or water, I took over the conversation, saying, "Look, gentlemen, I'm late for a dinner date and short on time." Then pointing to the car on the showroom floor, I said, "I want to buy that car. It is exactly what I have been looking for. I will give you a $10,000 down payment, and I want to pay off the balance in thirty-six months or less without a penalty." Handing the salesman my business card, I continued, "Call me at nine o'clock tomorrow morning and let me know the price and payments. My present car is coming off lease and I have to make a decision tomorrow."

I waited until noon the next day and no call from the salesman. I called another dealer in another town and described the exact car I wanted. After listening to me, he explained that he did not have that specific car in stock but would try to find one in the dealer network.

With this information, I told him where he would find the car I wanted, explaining the episode of the previous night. He made a dealer trade and I bought the car, but not from the salesman I asked to call me the next morning.

Several days later the telephone rang. It was the salesman I had asked to call me the next morning. I explained to him that I had bought the car that was in his showroom but that I had bought it from another dealer.

When I asked why he had not called, here was his classic response, "Well, I forgot that it was my day off. I wasn't at work that day."

Small wonder the automobile business is on the skids. They have forgotten how to sell, communicate, and inspire people to buy. Whatever happened to responsibility and integrity? If American manufacturers want to maximize sales efficiency and stop wasting money, they should begin to analyze what selling really is and how its effectiveness can be enhanced. Stop concentrating on "The Deal," start "Selling Solutions" and move a notch above being just a salesperson and become a *Professional Purchase Advisor (PPA)*.

A PPA is a consultant who counsels people on the value of making wise and intelligent buying decisions. PPAs are problem solvers. The product they represent offers a solution to a problem and in so doing adds value over price.

Customers want to engage with professionals who know their product or service, who understand and are responsive to their needs, and who are capable of communicating value over price. Price is the money you pay for the product or service; value is the benefit you receive from using it. Customers will always concentrate on price until the focus is changed to show how the benefits contribute extra value. Price is not a prime motivator. When the sales concentration is on price, it is an open invitation to shop the competition for a better price.

Goods and services do not have any intrinsic value; they only convey benefits to the user. Conveying benefits and value is the prime job of the sales communicator. Making a sale benefits both parties to the transaction, the buyer and the seller. The buyer enjoys the benefits buying the product provides and the seller enjoys the money he makes. Selling is a fun business.

No two people are exactly alike. Each is an individual; each has his or her unique and personal characteristics. Contrary to popular belief, people are not born with the talent to be in sales. Great sales communicators discover how to achieve dominion over themselves and become proficient in the profession of selling.

Believe it or not, you have the power to open new horizons for yourself and become a Professional Purchase Advisor.

There are just two basic qualities that you should possess to achieve success in the selling profession to become a Professional Purchase Advisor.

Number 1 is *empathy* and number 2 is *desire*.

Empathy is the ability to feel as the other person feels and to understand their emotions. This gives you the advantage so you can achieve mutual understanding and mutual satisfaction. With empathy you can sense the reactions of the person to whom you are talking and quickly adjust favorably to them. When you sense what the other person is feeling, you can change your pace and make adjustments that can lead to understanding and agreement with each other. In all communications it is vital to be able to sense what the other person is feeling and to change course and make modifications to make you a winner in a conversation or in making a sale.

Next is *desire* (this might also be called ego or drive). This is manifest in a burning desire to win, not merely for the money, but, simply, for the joy of being a winner. Money is a powerful motivator, but it is a proven fact that the desire for power, the exalted feeling of being a winner, is the overriding motivator. Money runs a close second.

Recognized leaders in business, politics, sports, and the professions achieved the pinnacle of their careers because they had a gnawing hunger and a driving desire to excel. Money was not their prime motivation. Money came as a result of their accomplishments.

Success enhances the ego and failure diminishes it. But the ego must be strong enough to be motivated by failure, not shattered by it.

An intense *desire* to be a winner coupled to *empathy* for your fellow man is a winning combination for a successful and satisfying career in sales and communications. Any man or woman who has a profound feeling of empathy and a burning inner desire and drive to be a winner has maximum motivation and will excel in sales, regardless of the product or service they represent. The only caveat is you must ask yourself, "Do I believe without reservation that this product or service will deliver real and specific benefits to the buyer?" If your answer is yes, you can sell it.

If you are blessed with a fine-tuned empathy but lack the fire of inner drive, you are probably a very nice, well-liked person. You are blessed with friends who trust and respect your judgment. In sales you would be attentive and focused on the customer's needs rather than your own desire to close the sale. Many people appreciate this personal concern.

On the other hand, if you are overly assertive and aggressive, you may have too much drive and too little empathy for others. In sales you might have a tendency to barge ahead and in the process irritate and close the mind and the pocketbook of the customer. Others find this kind of behavior challenging and find great satisfaction in matching wits with the aggressor.

The ability to sell is a uniquely human skill. Also, the ability to sell is a totally non-mechanical aptitude. Psychological testing seems only to indicate interest, and interest is not a test of ability. However, testing can reveal in which direction your personality leans.

All human beings fall into three temperament classes. These are:

- *The Extrovert.* This person is more concerned with action than with causes, expresses emotions outwardly, is outgoing and assertive, and likes to put ideas to action, often regardless of the consequences. These people are actors, politicians, salespeople, and athletes. If you were an extrovert, you would be very successful selling to similar types as you are. Extroverts find it fun to match words and wits with people of the same temperament.

  However, as salespeople they are often too assertive and aggressive, lacking the patience and finesse to handle difficult sales situations skillfully and diplomatically.

- *The Introvert.* This person prefers detailed work, likes to see concrete results of his or her own efforts, is concerned with causes, and gives careful analyses to all actions. These people usually are thinkers involved in such areas as engineering, accounting, and science. If you were an introvert, you would find a sales position selling products or services to other people sharing your temperament personally and financially rewarding. Introverts possess all requisites for successful sales careers.

- *The Ambivert.* This person is a balance of the two extremes and is capable of adjusting easily to situations. They have empathy for the feeling of others and have the drive to be a winner in dealing with people. This type would make good managers, teachers, executives, salespeople, and parents. If you possess these qualities, you have the skills, the empathy, and the drive to be successful selling any product or service to any or all of the three temperament groups.

Desire is the most pervasive human force. It is a smoldering fire inside you that will not let you sleep. It dominates your mind and body to do or to be something that will make a difference in your life.

Desire cannot be tested. The president of the University of Minnesota, a university renowned for aptitude testing, once remarked, "All of my life I have had an overpowering desire to become the president of a major university. I was tested for my aptitude to hold such a job, and the test revealed I lacked the necessary aptitudes. Psychologists tell us that testing cannot reveal the power of desire."

I have heard it said that bourbon whiskey was the antidote for rattlesnake bite, the only qualification being that the bourbon had to be in you when you were bitten. The same is true for *desire*. The fire must be in you to want to rise above the crowd.

12 How to Jump-Start Your Career . . . and Your Life

The reasonable man adapts himself to the world. The unreasonable man persists in trying to adapt the world to himself. Therefore all progress depends on the unreasonable man.

—George Bernard Shaw

The fault, dear Brutus, is not in our stars, but in ourselves, that we are underlings.

—William Shakespeare

If you are reading this book, I assume you want to rise above the average and to stand out from the crowd. You want to use your unique talents to be recognized as a leader in everything you do. You want to be able to command more money with the confidence that you can thrive in any economic recession.

If these assumptions fit, you are either a salesperson wanting to improve your skills as a *Professional Purchase Advisor* or a person searching for a new direction and control of your life. And if you have read this far, I assume you are interested in becoming a *Master Communicator.* Be assured, you are on the right track because the future does belong to the communicator.

The one hundred years of the twenty-first century will see unprecedented and exciting innovations and discoveries in technology, science, geopolitics, demographics, medicine, and the military.

New ideas and innovations, along with changes in the economy and the family structure, will not only create wealth but also will open new horizons of opportunities for men and women who want to be involved in bringing the good things of life to others. These exciting discoveries will be equally balanced with challenges that will require infinite wisdom, valor, justice, leadership, and statesmanship. It's going to be a wonderful time to be alive and to be a part of a solution.

What is discovered must be produced and distributed before its value can be appreciated. This requires the services of skilled sales communicators. As I have said many times in this book already, nothing happens until somebody sells something.

To give you inspiration about the future, look around yourself, in your home, in your car, at work. What hi-tech conveniences do you see: high-definition television; the wireless computer that connects you in seconds to the Internet that, in turn, connects you to the world; the cell phone that takes pictures as well as sends and receives text messages; voice mail; air conditioning; energy cells. And the list goes on and on, yet these inventions only occurred within the last seventy-five years.

More and more new technology is being introduced each day. Some of these ideas include automobile braking sensors that will stop your car before an accident happens and rear-view mirrors that will reveal two lanes of traffic on each side of your car to give you added safety. Many of these exciting new ideas and innovations will stir the imagination and create a desire to have and enjoy. The power that brings good ideas to the market lay in the talents of salespeople to communicate the good news. Nothing good comes to life until somebody communicates the good news.

We enjoy longer life and better health today because of medicine and experiments developed and practiced many years ago:

- Natives of Wales treated dropsy with an herb tea made from foxglove. Scientists have since discovered that foxglove contains digitalis, which is now used to increase the cardiac output in people suffering from heart failure.
- The snakeroot called Rauwolfia was used as medicine in ancient India. In 1940, it was discovered to have great value in treating heart disease.
- For many years New Englanders used May apples as an antidote

for warts. It has since been discovered that they do contain an anti-tumor substance.

- Bark from the willow tree is the basis for aspirin.
- South African natives used extract from jack-in the-pulpit plants as a contraceptive. This is the basis for "the pill" today.

The benefits of these folk medicines were not readily accepted until skilled communicators persuaded people of their value.

Many important discoveries have been made by mistake. This has been given a wonderful name: *Serendipity*. This is the effect by which one accidentally discovers something fortunate while looking for something else.

Serendipitous discoveries have been made in every discipline: pharmacy, medicine, science, economics, religion, chemistry, physics and astronomy. They include Teflon, Velcro, Scotchguard, cellophane, iodine, microwaves, electromagnetism, rubber, chocolate chip cookies, Post-it Notes, pacemakers and air conditioning (discovered while searching for a cure for malaria). The iPod was a mistake. It was discovered when the wrong microchip was used in a NASA onboard computer. The principle behind an inkjet printer was discovered when an engineer, by accident, put a hot soldering iron on his pen. A few seconds later ink was ejected from the pen's point. The microwave oven was discovered while testing a magnetron for radar sets. The engineer noticed that a peanut candy bar in his pocket melted when exposed to radar waves.

On a beautiful summer day in 1948, an amateur Swiss mountaineer and inventor named George de Mestra took his dog for a nature hike. Returning home he noticed that his wool pants and his dog were matted with burrs, the plant seed-sacs that cling to animal fur. Being an inventor and filled with curiosity, George de Mestral put the burrs under his microscope and discovered that they contained tiny hooks that made them cling so tenaciously to the small loops of fur on the dog and the tiny loops on the wool in his pants. He called his invention Velcro. Today it is a multimillion dollar industry—not too bad for a serendipitous invention based on Mother Nature.

These revolutionary discoveries in communications, travel, and technology were not readily accepted. It took the imagination and the drive of salespeople to make these good things of life available to everyone.

Coca-Cola was a classic mistake. An itinerant doctor had concocted a tonic to cure everything internally and externally. The doc was down on his luck and sold the formula for a few hundred dollars to a young pharmacist. The pharmacist added a few other ingredients and the result was Coca-Cola. Today, "Coke" is recognized worldwide.

Think of the wealth this product has produced and the value it has added to the economy in transportation, distribution, and jobs. A $500 investment by a pharmacist burgeoned into billions of dollars. Skilled sales communicators made these good things happen and became wealthy because of it.

Another mistake that has saved countless lives is penicillin. This was discovered when Alexander Fleming failed to disinfect cultures of bacteria when he was leaving on vacation. When he returned he found them contaminated with penicillium mold, which killed the bacteria. Millions of people are living healthy and productive lives today because skilled communicators brought this mistake to life by communicating its benefits and value.

Ivory, *"the soap that floats,"* is another household favorite discovered by mistake. James Gamble and his business partner, Harley Procter, left for lunch one day, leaving the air blower going in their newly processed vat of soap. When they returned, they discovered the soap had filled with air. Not wanting to waste the entire mix, they molded it into soap bars and discovered the soap would float. Being idea men, the soap was named Ivory and given the tag line, "It floats because it is 99 and 44/100% pure."

Skilled sales, merchandising, and advertising communicators launched this mistake to success in the market. Ivory soap had a unique advantage: it floated in the bathtub and was never out of sight. Of course, it was never revealed that any soap would float if enough air were pumped into it. Procter & Gamble built an empire on this mistake.

My good friend, Jim Gamble, namesake of the founder, shared this mistake with me. I believe it is true, but Jim had a sly twinkle in his eye when he told me this tale. Good marketing and salesmanship were the keystones of Procter & Gamble's success. Like everything available in the marketplace, you can discover a product, design it, produce it, market it, and advertise it. But nothing happens until somebody sells it.

Among the many quotations attributed to Thomas Edison, two are most appropriate for this chapter. Referring to mistakes and discoveries he made, he remarked:

I have failed my way to success many times.

And:

The trouble with most people is they quit before they start (or they quit the first time they fail).

Stop for just a minute to think about this: Would it not be better for you to have failed in everything you do than to have done absolutely nothing at all?

The writer James Joyce made a most appropriate remark when he said, "Mistakes are the portals for discovery." Louis Pasteur, a French chemist, made another powerful observation when he said, "Where opportunity is concerned, chance favors only the prepared mind."

The lessons to be learned from these remarks are that you should carefully look at your life: Study what you have done right, what you have done wrong and identify the alternatives you might have chosen. Then, when the time is right and the chance presents itself, you will be primed and ready to take advantage of whatever good opportunity comes your way. If you are ready, you may discover things you never thought of looking for and maybe an idea that could change you life for the better. When *serendipity* appears, you will be able to seize the moment and show that *it is never too late to jump-start your life.*

This is exactly what William Wrigley, Jr., did. Wrigley's name is synonymous with chewing gum: Spearmint, Juicy Fruit, and Doublemint gum, among others. Wrigley's rise to fame is a classic example.

Expelled from grammar school, William was put to work in the family business. His family manufactured a scouring soap and eventually he worked his way up to head of sales. To boost his sales of soap, Wrigley offered baking soda as a premium. Soon customers were asking for more baking soda than scouring soap. So, what else to do but go into the baking soda business? To boost sales of baking soda Wrigley offered sticks of chewing gum. Once again, more people asked for the chewing gum than baking soda. So, he went into the chewing gum business.

The rest is history. The sales of a nickel package of gum made Wrigley one the richest men in America. He parlayed his five-cent package of chewing gum into an empire that at one time owned the Chicago Cubs baseball team and the legendary Wrigley Field. He owns an entire island off the coast of California named Catalina. The Wrigley building in Chicago is a tourist landmark and an architectural treasure. Not bad for a kid who was expelled from grammar school!

J.C. Penney of department store fame is another example of "it's never too late to jump-start your life." Late in life he was financially disabled and in poor health, but he picked himself up and started all over again, building his little store into a retailing icon. *Fortune* named the J.C. Penney "The Most Admired General Merchandise Store." It is interesting to note the initials in Penney's name: "J" is for James and the "C" is for the name Cash. James Cash Penney was once quoted as saying, "Give me a stock clerk with a goal, and I will give you a man who will make history. But give me a man with no goal, and I will give you a stock clerk."

Each of these personal stories personifies the magic of serendipity changing and jump-starting lives. This can happen to you, too.

Dr. William C. Menninger, the world-famous psychiatrist, asks the personal question, "Do you know where you want to go? Most important, do you know whether or not you are going in the right direction?"

If you are not happy with the direction your life has taken—if you desire more money, a better position, more recognition, enhanced prestige, and a solid feeling of accomplishment that your job and your life is really fulfilling—now—not tomorrow, but today—is the time to take control of your life. Yesterday is gone, tomorrow is yet to come. Now is the only moment you have to take action.

I would like to suggest you insert some *serendipity* into your life. Stick out your neck and begin searching your environment for those things that fulfill everything your wildest imagination has envisioned for you. What have you dreamed of doing or having that you have not done or do not now have?

Jackie Cochran, American Woman Aviator was one of the most gifted women racing pilots in the world. Serendipitous chance opened a career in aviation for her.

Tragedy marred the early years of her life; her four-year old son died a horrible death after setting his clothes on fire. Following her divorce Jackie found a job as a hairdresser in a beauty salon. One day a friend offered her a ride in his airplane; this ride changed her life. Jackie was hooked on flying. She was so thrilled that she learned to fly and earned her pilot's license after only two short weeks of training. Jackie was a natural pilot. She went on to earn her commercial pilot's license.

The rest is history. Flying was her obsession. She was the first woman to take off from an aircraft carrier, the first woman to reach Mach 2, the first woman to pilot a bomber across the Atlantic, the first woman to make a blind (instrument) landing, the first woman to fly a fixed wing, jet aircraft across the Atlantic, The first woman to break the sound barrier flying at 652 mph. Jackie was the first pilot to fly above 20,000 feet with an oxygen mask and the first woman to enter the Bendix transcontinental Race. She holds more distance and speed records than any pilot living or dead, male or female.

During World War II she organized the Women's Air Force Service Pilots—better knows as WASP. This group of women pilots ferried bombers and fighter planes across the Atlantic Ocean to our troops overseas.

Cochran was an organizer, a master communicator and persuasive motivator. She left this inspirational message for future generations of women: "If you will open up your power plants of vitality and energy, clean up your spark plugs of ambition and desire and pour in the fuel of work you will be likely to go places and do things."

Condoleezza Rice comes naturally by her skills as a master communicator. Her mother was a science, music and oratory teacher, and her father was an ordained Westminster Presbyterian minister; both careers require the skills of a master communicator. Condoleezza learned them well. Her roots date back to the pre-Civil War where her family worked as sharecroppers in the Southern States.

Her career goal was to become a concert pianist, but serendipity stepped in. She changed her mind about a career after she attended a course in international relations taught by Josef Korbel, the father of future Secretary of State Madeline Albright.

Rice was the second woman after Albright to serve as Secretary of State. She served as Secretary of State under George W. Bush. World leaders discovered her to be a shrewd leader with formidable political skills. As Secretary of State she was third in line to be President of the United States.

She earned the right to be called a master communicator and to be recognized as a "Statesman."

Be honest in your answer to these questions: How many times have you really wanted to have something and did your best to get it, but you failed because it was just a little beyond your reach? Did you just give up and quit? Or did you learn from your mistakes and then dig in with determination and give it another try? Henry Ford once said, "Failure is simply the opportunity to begin again more intelligently." He should have known. He went bankrupt several times before achieving success.

Do you really want to get the things you have never had but envision having in your dreams? If you do, maybe it is time for you to begin doing the things that you have never done before to get what you desire.

Emily Dickinson lived her entire life within herself. She was incredibly shy; she never left the confines of her home to travel or to experience the real world. She lived in her imagination, where her mind generated vivid associations. Although she had never experienced living in the actual world, she wrote over 1,700 poems in which she vividly described the human experience. But Emily sent a message to us all when she wrote: "Imagination lights the slow fuse of the possible."

Your imagination has created mental pictures for you of things you have never experienced but desire to have. If you want to bring the things you envision to the reality of the present, it is important to build a bridge strong enough to make it happen. All you need do is persuade yourself that you will make it happen. Nothing will happen until you sell yourself. Jobs will come and go, but the one constant in your life is your talent to adapt.

Are you equal to the task ahead? If you have confidence that you are, then begin building the bridge from where you are to where you want to be. In the process you will discover that the seeds of success are sown in the oddest of places. Somewhere in the Good Book we are admonished: "Seek and you shall find." A wiser man than I said that.

Maybe, just maybe, in the process you will discover, whether by accident and sagacity, the right niche for you. In the process, I am confident you will discover that being a master communicator will give a new burst of enthusiasm and a sense of accomplishment. Give serendipity a chance.

History tells us that Christopher Columbus set out to find a trade route to the East Indies and, by mistake, discovered America. Like Columbus, you have nothing to lose and everything to gain. When you become a master communicator you just might discover the treasure you have pictured in your imagination.

Albert Einstein, Nobel prize-winning physicist, had a formula for success. Being interviewed at the height of his career, he was asked, "What is your secret for success?" Einstein replied, "Read fairy tales." The interviewer, caught off-guard by the terseness of his unconventional answer, probed deeper, "Anything else?" Einstein replied, "Yes, read more fairy tales. Fairy tales stir our imaginations to dream the impossible dream."

Einstein dreamed about discovering the forces that control the universe. He combined his dreams with his vivid imagination and converted them to action in theoretical physics. His discoveries have changed the concept of the universe.

What are your dreams? Where does your imagination take you? Go forward with confidence in the direction of your dreams and live your life as you imagine you would like it to be. When you challenge yourself to do this you will be rewarded with uncommon success. Einstein added another thought to ponder: "Imagination is the preview of life's coming attractions."

One constant thread is woven into the lives of all successful people. Everyone has a self-defined goal that directs all of their energies. Andrew Carnegie, many years ago, made the comment: "No one can acquire riches or material things without having a clear mental picture of the things one seeks. Success demands that you have a definite purpose." What is the goal *you* want to accomplish?

Life is a journey of discoveries. If you are blessed with an imagination and a desire to rise above the crowd, you have had many fantastic journeys. These are the times when you imagined having money, health, good relationships, and happiness in every corner of your life. During these journeys you visualized the untapped, hidden power within you.

Did you ever awaken in the middle of one of these dreams? Immediately you closed your eyes tightly and tried to pick up where the dream left off. Dreams can be made to come true. Walt Disney's creations of Mickey Mouse, Disneyland, and Disney World is proof positive that dreams can come true.

There is a wonderful book written by Rhonda Byrne called *The Secret*. The book contains secrets that have been passed down through the centuries, secrets that have been understood by some of the most prominent people in history, such as Plato, Galileo, Beethoven, Edison, Carnegie, Einstein, and other great thinkers.

I would like to quote from the Introduction,

> As you learn The Secret, you will come to know how you can have, be, or do anything you want. You will come to know who you really are. You will come to know the true magnificence that awaits you in life.

The book is truly inspirational.

The very best place to begin planning for a change of direction in your life is your mind. *Visualize* the end result you want to achieve. Jack "The Bear" Nicklaus (the professional golfer who dominated the championship ranks in the 1960s and 1970s, winning twenty championship titles), was asked by a reporter, "Jack, what is your secret for being as winner?" Jack's answer was, "Every time before I swing my club, I visualize the exact spot where I expect the ball to land. I rivet this solidly in my mind. Only then do I swing the club, and the ball generally lands where I planned it would land."

Decide where you want to go in your life, where you want to be, and what you want to do. Once this goal is riveted in your mind, you can plan how you are going to get from where you are to where you want to be. This will be an exploratory mission and along the way you may discover by accident the elusive treasure that will change your life.

Keep your mind open to discovering that becoming a master communicator may fill your life's treasure chest.

Good sales communications are the steam turbines that keep the wheels of industry and our economy vibrant and moving forward. Stop to think for a minute! How many jobs would you as a salesperson generate when you close a sale? Experts estimate that the average salesperson provides work for sixty-nine people. By generating new customers and retaining the business from old customers, employment is sustained for twenty-five factory workers, nineteen workers in offices and on farms get paychecks, and the remaining twenty-five have direct or indirect jobs as suppliers or vendors in the channels of distribution— all because of the orders produced by people who earn their living in sales.

Imagine this: Every time you made a sale somebody would buy something, and this would move the economy forward—providing jobs, income, profit, and a better standard of living for all to enjoy. You would have a very important job, plus a very healthy income.

According to the U.S. Department of Labor, there are 153,516,000 people in the labor force (October 2007). A select, talented few are salesmen and saleswomen persuading people to purchase the products and services that have been produced. All the other workers are selling the value of their work to management in hopes of getting a promotion and earning more money. Even the CEOs of corporations are selling the value of their savvy to their boards of directors. Everyone is in sales, selling himself or herself to someone else.

There are thirteen million businesses in the USA; every one of them needs customers and profitable sales to survive. Every business is hungry for sales leadership. Every business has its up and down cycles. In bad periods workers are retired or let go, but good salespeople never lose their jobs; they are the vital link between profit and loss. Good salespeople always make good money; and great salespeople always make great money.

All it takes for you to be a great sales communicator is faith in yourself, a positive, optimistic attitude, and a product or service in which you believe. Add a dash of imagination, a sprinkle of empathy, and a splash of desire to be successful and enjoy what you do. If you enjoy earning money and having the time of your life, become a master sales communicator—you'll like it.

We are all selling something—a product, a service, or ourselves. So why not construct a moneymaking career for yourself by becoming a master communicator and a professional purchase advisor to customers and a business builder for your company? I don't know of a better way to earn money.

Decide today that you are going to raise yourself above the crowd. Decide how much money you want to make so you can enjoy all the good things you have ever wished for or imagined. There is a tremendous feeling of power in being able to acquire things, even apart from the anticipation of enjoying what was acquired.

Right now, while visions of the money you're going to earn is fresh and flashing in your mind, get a pencil and a piece of paper, get yourself a Coke or a cup of coffee, sit in a comfortable chair at a desk or table, relax, and follow this arithmetic:

> Jot down how much money you paid income taxes on last year—your gross income, not net after taxes.

Underneath this figure write the money you would like to earn next year. Please be realistic, don't write one million dollars unless you plan to win the lotto or a rich relative is going to will it to you. Be practical, be realistic and be specific. Do not say, "I want to make more money." Be specific: Exactly how much money and what for. What do you feel you would like to earn?

There are fifty-two weeks in a year, and you work forty hours a week; 40 times 52 equals 2,080 working hours a year.

Subtract 80 hours for two weeks vacation. That leaves you with 2,000 working hours.

From the 2,000 hours subtract coffee and potty breaks, travel time and just plain goofing off time. Time management experts tell us this amounts to 648 hours. Subtract 648 from 2,000, and you have 1,352 hours of productive working time. Now comes the revelation. Divide the money you want to earn by the 1,352 working hours, and you will have the dollar value of every hour you work.

To earn $200,000 next year, you must generate $147.93 each working hour. To earn $100,000, you need to earn $73.96. If your goal is $75,000, you should produce $55.47 per hour.

These figures are only if you are self-employed. If you are working for a corporation, add fifty cents to each dollar to accommodate benefits management pays to you. Woody Hays, legendary coach of Ohio State for many years, once remarked, "The only things that are the same in this world are the number of hours in a day. The difference in winning or losing is what you do with those hours." What do you do with those hours? Professional communicators make every hour pay.

I have devoted the pages of this book to the techniques that will make you a skilled communicator, the practice of which will make you a winner in dealing with people. The logical transition as a skilled communicator is to move into sales because this is where you can really make money and have fun helping people live more fully with the products you have sold them.

You might ask, "How can I become a better communicator or how can I launch a career in sales?" The techniques of selling have remained constant, but the high-pressure tactics of years past have faded. High-pressure selling is a crude relic of bygone days. Generally, it is thought of as bullying or tricking a person into buying something he cannot afford, does not need, does not want, or will leave him totally dissatisfied with the salesman and the company who persuaded him to buy—and irritated at himself for having bought it.

Today the objective of salesmanship is to let the buyer sell himself. This concept does not diminish or negate the power of salesmanship. It is simply selling with kid gloves instead of boxing gloves. "Reason Why" salesmanship is skillfully communicating to the buyer or customer all of the reasons why it would be to his benefit to buy now.

This is where communication skills become the tipping point. By communicating the benefits of buying so clearly and cogently, the customer knows he has made a wise decision without an afterthought that he has been sold something he doesn't need, want, or cannot afford.

Selling works for society when the person doing the selling and the person doing the buying are both wholly satisfied with the results. Good relationships are established for future sales and best of all is when satisfied customers recommend their friends and associates to purchase from you.

Selling can be adversarial, but at its best selling is complementary. Both parties benefit when a favorable relationship is formed. This makes a job in sales very satisfying and also great fun.

In my early days of sales training, I learned all the "tricks" that tended to make selling adversarial. As a teenage boy selling door to door, I had a problem getting the lady of the house to open the door. This was in the day when doors had a small peephole at the top. The lady of the house would open the peephole and see a man she did not know and wouldn't open the door. When I explained my dilemma to my boss, he gave me five dollars and directed me to go buy a hat.

The next day when I rang the doorbell, I put my hat over the peephole in the door. The lady of the house, seeing total darkness, would quickly open it. I had an audience in front of me, albeit an irritated one. Nevertheless, it was a live body.

Ladies in sales had another ploy to get a sympathetic audience. Before ringing a doorbell they would buy a string of faux pearls. When the lady of the house opened the door, the string of pearls would suddenly break, sending a cascade of pearls rolling across the floor. Both the customer and the saleslady were quickly on their hands and knees retrieving the pearls. The saleslady had a very empathetic audience.

I took every sales course and attended every inspirational sales rally by every speaker—from Elmer Wheeler ("Sell the Sizzle, not the Steak") to Bill Gove, Larry Wilson, Ken McFarland, Zig Ziglar and many others. I learned every kind of sales opener, all the action words to grab attention, and every closing technique from the *Assumptive Close* to the *Puppy Dog Close* to the *Alternative Close*, the *45 Caliber Close* and the *Picture the Future Close*—all good tactics, but the execution sounded contrived unless used with finesse and polish. Top-level salespeople know and use these tactics, but they temper and adapt them to a personal style of communicating.

These sales rallies and motivational speeches were great training sessions. The speakers were stem-winders and motivators. I would leave their sessions full of juice, charged and ready to conquer the most irascible old curmudgeon of a buyer. Commenting on the value of motivation, one student made the comment, "Motivation is only a passing surge of energy. It doesn't last." Zig Ziglar responded with, "Okay, you're right, but I say that bathing doesn't last either. That's why I recommend doing it daily." Everyone from time to time needs a shot of inspiration to keep them moving in the right direction.

I did have one customer named Carl who was an irascible old curmudgeon. He was a bully who took great delight in finding ways to demoralize me. It was a game with him. I should have stood up to him and said enough is enough, but I played right into his hands. He not only gave me a bad time, he was giving me ulcers. I decided to call his bluff and to get rid of him as a customer.

One morning after taking his abuse, I looked him right in the eye (which is the wrong thing to do unless you want a fight) and said, "Carl, I only wish that I had two customers just like you!"

He let my remark settle into his mind. With his forehead quizzically wrinkled, he looked at me and said, "You wish you had two customers like me? Come on now. I know I'm tough on you, but I know you don't want another customer who will give you nothing but trouble." I let a smile cross my face and told him, "You're right, Carl. I've got three disagreeable customers just like you—and I wish I only had two." He laughed and came over and put his arm around my shoulder, saying, "Bob, you are the only salesman with guts enough to call my bluff." He became my best customer.

I learned how to handle a bully or a high-gear-type buyer from a guy named Sam Vinning. Sam was a sales trainer and motivational speaker for Westinghouse. His advice was that to be successful in sales you had to learn when to quit and when to stay and fight for the sale (same as in a game of poker, you have to know when to hold and when to fold).

Sam's advice was to leave the tough ones to your competition; they'll harass and give your competitors a bad time instead of you. While your competitors are wasting their time on the tough ones, you have a field of good customers open for you to sell.

The inspiring words of these sales motivators sparked a fire in me to earn money and be successful. This fire was a powerful force. I practiced to perfect my techniques on every sales call I made. One time a good customer on whom I was practicing stopped me and jokingly remark, "Bob, from the words you are using I can tell that you've taken the Elmer Wheeler sales course. Every salesman calling on me sounds like a puppet on a string mouthing and mimicking the techniques of the sales gurus." He admonished me to knock it off: "Don't put up a false façade—just be yourself."

This man was a good friend. He possessed the wisdom garnered with age and a lifetime of experience. He counseled me, saying, "Bob, every human being is intended to have a character of his own. You can be what no other is, and you can do what no other can do."

He continued with another bit of fatherly advice, saying, "If you follow the crowd and copy others, you'll get no farther than the crowd. But if you walk alone and be your own man, you will find yourself in places no one has ever been before." Then he added one more piece of sage wisdom, saying, "When you stand out from the crowd, you will add distinction to your life."

There are several men who stand out from the crowd because they have done something no man has ever done before. They landed and walked on the moon. The Apollo 11 crew, Command module pilot Michael Collins; Edwin Aldrin Jr, lunar module pilot; and Neil Armstrong. The first man to stand on the moon was Neil Armstrong. He said the historic words, "One small step for man, one giant leap for mankind." A camera in the lunar module provided live television coverage to the entire world as Armstrong climbed down the ladder to the surface of the moon.

Our insatiable curiosity about the earth, the moon, the sun, the stars and other galaxies in the solar system will drive the United States into new exploration of the universe in which we live. Men and women who want to stand out from the crowd will step forward to become astronauts and discover whether or not there is life in the universe. Sally Ride stepped forward and became the first woman in space; there will be more to follow on Sally Ride.

Sandra Day O'Connor is a quietly determined woman who has stepped out of the ordinary to blaze new trails for her sex; she has become a roll model for Americans of both sexes and all ages. In 1981 President Ronald Reagan nominated her to the Supreme Court. She became the court's 102nd member and the first female member. She retired after 24 years of service on the bench.

The question waiting for your answer is, "How do you stand out from the crowd?" Every person has his or her unique style and personality. You are an individual and you have unique talents and strengths that you were born with and that remain unchanged throughout your life. This might explain why every so often, when you are dissatisfied with your lot, you mentally lash out at yourself, crying, "Why, why do I just sit here working 8 to 5 at this lousy job when I was born to be successful and wealthy?" Maybe you were born for a career in sales.

Discovering who and what you are will be the pivot point in your life. It will unleash the boundless power you have to turn your life in any direction you want, and it will be your key to successful personal relationships and to your career development. It is up to you: Use it or lose it.

Let's take a look at a couple of United States army generals to make the point. Both had four stars on their shoulders and battle ribbons on their chests. Both were decorated successful leaders of men in combat. But they were 180-degree opposites in demeanor and disposition. Their names? Omar Bradley and George S. Patton.

Patton was born to battle. He was brash, controversial, outspoken, and opinionated. Bradley was polite, gentle, and courteous. He was known as the "soldier's general" and never gave an order without prefacing it with the word "Please."

Patton and Bradley had a common trait: Each man was dedicated to his job as a leader, and each respected the men they led. Both accepted full responsibility for their decisions, yet each stood out from the crowd in his own, distinctive way.

How do you stand out from the crowd? What differentiates you from your friends, relatives, neighbors, and business associates?

Think about it. Omar Bradley was a gentle man. He wore conservative uniforms and was not ostentatious in his dress or his actions. He projected refinement. On the other hand, George Patton was a ramrod, and he dressed the part. His uniforms reinforced his image. He always wore polished cavalry boots. A pearl-handled revolver was strapped to each hip, and he used a swagger stick to punctuate his pit bulldog image, which was his favorite breed of dog.

What is the unique point of difference that sets you apart from the ordinary? Is there anything unusual in your physical appearance? If you are unusually short, tall, fat, or skinny, you are probably remembered as Shorty, Slim, Chub, or Bones. At least you have a visible point of difference.

If you do not have any visible features that differentiate you from the crowd, what are the favorable points of difference of your personality? Are you open to unusual ideas? Are you conscientious and self-disciplined? Do you seek the stimulation and the company of others? Are you compassionate and cooperative? A good balance of these personality traits is ideal for a career in sales and communications.

I would like to ask you a question. "What reason do you give yourself for getting out of bed each morning?" Is it drudgery to get up because you have a menial and tedious job to go to? When push comes to shove in your life, do you look at your job and question, "What am I really doing and where am I going? I'll never get rich slaving away as I am now doing."

Or, do you bounce out of bed every morning knowing that you have an exciting job that gives you a sense of purpose and satisfaction? Nothing is as invigorating as the realization that you are important in bringing good things to life for others and, in the process, banking a lot of money for yourself.

Harold G. Koenig, M.D., professor of psychiatry and behavioral sciences at Duke University, has been involved in some interesting studies. He points out that a growing body of research suggests that people who have a sense of purpose and who feel that their life is a part of a larger plan have stronger immune systems, lower blood pressure, a lower risk of heart attack and cancer, heal faster, and live longer.

What kind of job do you have? If you would like a job that is challenging, exciting and satisfying, give sales a try. It certainly will improve your capacity to earn money and in so doing will enhance your personal well-being. Try a job with real purpose, like a job in sales. Try it, you'll like it.

After a lifetime in sales I have come to the conclusion that every man and woman is born with the courage to accomplish and win anything he or she may desire and also is blessed with a creative imagination. The problem is that in our daily lives so very few of us are challenged to exercise our creativity and to test our courage. Many of us need a clarion call to wake us up to the potential that lies within us. The biggest personal obstruction to rising above the crowd is fear— fear of making the wrong decision, fear of ridicule, fear of rejection, fear of failing, fear of personal embarrassment.

I had a friend named Major Pappy Boyington, commander of the Black Sheep squadron in World War II and recipient of the Medal of Honor. Pappy was his own man. He was tough as they come and fearless. One day on a Pacific Island, just before a raid on enemy forces, one of his young pilots confessed to Pappy about his fear, not of flying but, rather, his fear that he might not perform well under fire, thereby letting down his buddies.

Without hesitation, Pappy punched the lieutenant in the jaw, knocking him to the ground. The stunned pilot sprang up like a coiled spring, both hands clenched, ready to fight. Pappy stopped him, saying, "See, Lieutenant, when you are in battle and the chips are down, fear will leave you and you will perform like the man you were born to be."

So where do you go to launch a career in sales, or wherever your dreams take you. so you can be the winner you were born to be? It is possible and very likely that you can find a job in sales without leaving your current employer.

Here's how.

Go to the person in your company who is responsible for selling the product or service your company produces. Suggest to this person, "I've got an idea for you. I am thoroughly sold on the product we produce. I know the problem it solves and the benefits it gives to customers. I am convinced that I can sell the product we make. I like this company, I like the people I work with and I'd like the opportunity to prove my worth to you in sales."

I'll bet you will receive a respectful reception. You will have an attentive audience. Now is the time to use you skills as a master communicator and persuader to sell your way into sales.

Sales opportunities abound today. I recently received a letter from a company whose product I have used for several years. The letter read: "As a good customer, you love shopping with us. You'll love working for us. We are looking for sales and management people. You are invited to become part of our team. We'd be delighted to have you join us. Interested? Call today."

This is only one of several letters I have received from other companies with whom I do business. All are inviting me to apply for a sales or management position or to recommend a friend I know who may be available for a new career. Every business and industry, from retail to science, is looking for skilled communicators.

Notice that I said *skilled communicators,* not salesmen. The reason is that managers have discovered that too many sales types have learned all the ploys that will not work any more. With this knowledge, they stay within the confines of the box in which they have been trained, never exercising any new ideas or innovations. Men and women who are trained communicators, however, aren't lazy. They use refreshing, new, and interesting approaches to selling with great success.

Many companies today do not use sales training programs that match new salespeople with sales veterans. They have discovered that this association "watch-and-learn" training is counterproductive. The trainees learn all the bad habits (as well as some of the good habits) of the seasoned salespeople. The result: they have a sales staff of look-a-likes and act-a-likes, but not real salespeople.

The new approach to sales training is to let the new salespeople train themselves. The company sets the job and product requirements, sets goals and quotas, and monitors reviews of performance. The salespeople are on their own, using new ideas, techniques, and approaches to generate sales in their own inimitable way.

Do you buy products and services that give you great satisfaction? If you are sold on the product, knowing from experience the value it gives you, then, using your persuasive communication skills, you can sell it to others. Ask for an interview with their manager of sales. This is not really selling, it is better known as sharing good ideas with others. You get the money and the other person gets the product (or service) that has more value to him than the money he pays to you. This is salesmanship 101, and it is a fine way to launch a sales career.

Another way to scout out sales opportunities is to use the Internet. Log onto *salesjobs.com, monster.com, hotjobs.com,* or *careerbuilder.com.* You'll find sales opportunities in over fifty different business classifications in any state or city of your choice. This is a veritable potpourri of valuable career information. You'll find job search information, career advice, resume writing hints, interview hints, and advice on what to wear when interviewing.

Read the newspapers, the "Help Wanted" ads, of course, but exercise some imagination and creativity. Scan the business section and read and scan the advertisements. When you read that a company is expanding or has done something newsworthy, pick up the telephone and call them, or send them a personal note congratulating them and telling them you like their company and product and feel you can add muscle to their sales arm. If you have a resume include this, too. Do these things and you lift yourself above the crowd. Let management know that you are different because you have ideas and imagination.

Be sure to read the trade journals, particularly journals of the business or industry for which you have an affinity. Look for industry problems and opportunities that you can be interested in and enthusiastic about. Then write or call the management of these companies and let them know of your interest.

I guarantee you: When you let management know that you have taken the time and the trouble to dig into their business concerns, you will have a receptive audience. This is how you can differentiate yourself from the crowd.

If you do not have a business card or a piece of personal identification showing your address, telephone number, and e-mail address, get one today. For a couple of dollars you can get a personal address card.

Every time you patronize a restaurant or other place of business, write a short note complimenting the service: "Thank you for making this time so enjoyable." This courtesy is so unusual and different from the norm of being quick to complain, but slow to compliment. Do this, and it will make you a winner in dealing with people.

Here is a classic example of consideration paying handsome dividends. One of my clients was a plastics company. Their business was producing a vast array of plastic products. One of products produced was a handle for brushes. One weekend we held an open house for customers and prospects to see a demonstration of new, state-of-the-art extrusion equipment. The plant was in a large industrial district, and at the noon hour two young boys rode by on their bicycles. Seeing the activity and as curious twelve-year-olds would do, they stuck their heads in the door and asked, "What's going on here today?"

The plant manager could have told them to get lost, but as he explained to me later, "The boys looked clean and they were courteous, so I invited them to come on in and take a look. Inviting the boys in was one of the best decisions I ever made." Then he went on to explain that during the following week he received a call from a neighboring manufacturer whose product was industrial brushes. After introducing himself, he explained the reason for his call, saying, "You were kind enough to show my two boys through your plant last Saturday. They were telling me the wonderful plastics you produced, and I thought plastic handles for my brushes might improve their marketability."

Well as a result of being nice to two young boys, my client's company received a million-dollar order to produce plastic handles for his neighbor's brushes. You never know where kindness will lead you. Does serendipity work? You bet it does.

Finally, this next suggestion will make you a winner in everything you do—in business, in your personal life and in every association you have with people. *Write the letter you do not have to write.* Compliment the deed, not the person, and you'll never be accused of insincere flattery.

Whenever a friend, customer or business associates does something credible and deserving of recognition, take time to send a personal note of congratulations. This will set you part from the crowd, and you will be remembered as a thoughtful, considerate individual.

The ideas and words of wisdom that have been presented to you in this book are the result of a lifetime spent in advertising and sales. If you are in sales, I hope you have discovered some ideas or thoughts that will sharpen your skills. If you are not in sales and I have been successful in making you want to explore being a master communicator as a new direction in your life, I will have fulfilled my goal.

Nothing happens until somebody sells something.

Ronald Reagan, the 40th President of The United States is well identified with the title, "The Great Communicator." His early life in the state of Iowa was as a sports broadcaster announcing football games. Then he moved to Chicago where he broadcast baseball games for the Chicago Cubs. Following a successful career as a movie actor in Hollywood he moved into Television as a host for the General Electric Theatre and finally as host for the TV series of Death Valley Days.

Finally his skills as a communicator propelled him to Governor of the State of California and finally to the White House as President of the United States. As President, one of his greatest challenges was the Berlin Wall. Here his strength as a sales persuader and as a Great Communicator made history around the world.

Speaking at the Berlin Wall in 1987 President Reagan challenged Gorbachev saying: "General Secretary Gorbachev, if you seek peace, if you seek prosperity for the Soviet Union and Eastern Europe, if you seek liberalization, come here to this gate! Mr. Gorbachev, open this gate! Mr. Gorbachev, ***tear down this wall!***"

I had the pleasure of talking to Ronald Reagan many years ago before he was President. It was at a meeting of the Advertising Club Of Los Angeles where his brother Neil Reagan was President of the club. In a casual exchange of words I asked him about his career. He responded to me with, "I'm in sales." Then he added, "I've always been selling something—football, baseball, movies, television shows. It's my life."

Of course, he went on to communicate his skills as an administrator to the people of the United States. President Ronald Reagan was a Great Communicator. He made good things come to life.

How about you?

FUN Change Your Life: Become a Communicator and Have FUN Doing It

If you are not excited about getting up out of bed and going to work every morning—quit, resign, give it up. Find a new direction and a financially rewarding purpose for your life. Take the first job in sales you can find, and step up the ladder of life to financial security and independence. Do this and you can retire with assurance that you will have a paycheck for the rest of your life.

Others have done it and, with your God-given talents, you can be a champion persuader and master communicator, too. All it takes is guts, drive and determination to rise above the crowd—sales skills can be practiced and perfected along the way.

At one point in my life, I hired a sales manager. It didn't take him long to earn the title *Sales Mangler.* He had one sales principle: "Go for the Jugular"—customer relations be damned; sell, sell, sell. He irritated customers, employees, and his sales staff. He had absolutely no finesse. He was like a bull in a china shop, and I had to send in the troops to pick up the pieces. Selling was a hit-and-run transaction. His sales principle was sell a product. Once the sale is made, you never see or hear from him again. The sale was a one-time transaction.

Today, selling is different. Few products and services have any intrinsic differences. They are commodities. The growing proliferation of products and competition points out that there is not a shortage of products, but there is a shortage of customers to buy the products. Skilled sales communicators who can add the value of service and confidence to the buying process are needed.

Selling in today's sales environment is not "Go for the Jugular." Today's customers want value, service, quality, honesty, and integrity, plus convenience and helpful communication. Great service, great products and helpful communications are what it takes to move people to buy.

Everyday of your life you deal with a wide range of varied personalities. To succeed you must have keen powers of perception. This is the ability to observe and analyze the personalities and character of the people you come in contact with in your daily work. For communicators and salespeople this is applied psychology and the art of influencing people's thinking and feelings.

The ability to size-up people, in a general way at least, enables you to gain a broader understanding of the other person. Knowing this, you can select the key that will fit the lock to harmonize with the temperament of each person with whom you come in contact.

This knowledge can be developed through conscious and keen observation—and certainly through continual practice to improve your skills and rise above the crowd.

When you stop to think about it, every person, customer or prospect must buy from someone. Why shouldn't it be you? They will buy from you if you take time to learn how to handle them the way they like to be handled. How about you, how do you like to be handled by salespeople? Everyday you are confronted with lousy examples of salesmanship that turn you off. Now think about the good examples that really turned you on and helped you make a wise decision. Copy the empathy and consideration of the good example and you are off to a running start to becoming a star sale performer.

Selling is easy and selling is fun. To me, every day selling or communicating with others is a fun-filled challenge. I have made a practice of classifying people—friends, acquaintances, buyers and customers included—into six broad classes. Every contact I make gives me an opportunity to test my skills. Often I meet an adversary as motivated to win as am I. This is when the game of communicating gets exciting and fun, especially when you win.

Here's how I classify people and buyers:

- *The high-geared type*—These people are impatient, they move fast and will interrupt you frequently. They want the broad outline, the big picture of the proposition first—the details can come later. They make decisions based on hunch or gut-feeling. They are risk-takers who act quickly and also dump you for a competitor just as fast. Generally they are high-strung and excitable. Handle this type quickly and quietly and never get in their way.

- *The low-geared type*—They are slow thinkers. They are conservative, deliberate and orderly. They want a lot of facts and evidence and they are opinionated. Handle these people tactfully with kid gloves. These people are super cautious, but they develop into good friends and customers when handled and serviced with patience and finesse.

- *Hard-boiled, decisive type*—These are the irascible curmudgeons, usually cynical and a bit sadistic. They enjoy a good verbal battle, but they do admire a brawler who fights back but doesn't deflate their ego. Win these people and you have a friend for life.

- *The milquetoast, indecisive type*—These people are afraid of making a mistake. They avoid saying "Yes" until they are sure what others have done. You must assure these people they are making a wise and intelligent decision by providing them with stories and examples to support their choice. Be quietly positive and narrow their decision down to just two things: Would you like this one or that one?

- *The strong silent type*—This type is usually cold and not-too-friendly. You'll find them a bit egotistical but intellectual with a critical and analytical mind. With this person you build a logical case and put the facts in writing. You cannot high-pressure this person. But, you can win him by using these three powerful selling words to play on his intellectual ego: "*As you know*, Mr. Jones . . ."

- *The good-natured love everybody type*—This person is the master at the brush-off and stalling tactics. This is a good-natured person, easy going and sociable. He is proud of his business and civic achievements and desires recognition. Handle this person with a pleasant manner, using sincere flattery to get action.

Character analysis is far from being a science. But if you will take time to Stop, Look and Listen to people, you will soon discover that people often wear masks of false faces in order to cover up inner personal fears and uncertainties—even as you and I do.

The Chinese have a proverb, "He who cannot smile ought not to keep shop." People who enjoy their work, who like to meet and greet people, who are cordial and considerate of the feelings of others and who have a sincere smile that comes from the heart—you will be welcomed warmly by all the people you meet.

Although this book was not intended as a manual of sales techniques, I would be remiss if I did not end with a short summary of what it takes to be a master communicator and successful salesperson. Here is how I recommend opening and handling a conversation or sales interview:

The opening. Have a rapier-fast, one-sentence opener that grabs attention and gives a valid reason why it will be worth the time to listen to you. The first impression you make is vital. Seldom do you get a second chance to make a first impression.

- *What do you have and what will it do for me?* Have an idea or information that will solve a problem. People are more interested in the benefits a product or service gives than the features that make the benefits possible.

- *What are the features that make the benefits possible?* Be certain you cover your complete story. Do not assume the other person knows all the facts. You cannot bore a listener; they just stop listening, so know when to change your pace. A one-page written resume with visuals to pass on is a good idea for ensuring that all bases are covered. What evidence do you have to reinforce what you say? Be armed with testimonials from satisfied customers and case histories from well-known users. Cover the reputation and the abilities of your company, quality and prices, and delivery and service facilities. Tell just enough to complete the transaction. Wise Voltaire observed, "The secret to being a bore is to tell everything."

- *Get the customer or prospect in the act.* Check your progress by asking questions like, "What is your opinion?" Use the first person "you," not "we." People are interested in their own problems and welfare, not yours. Ask questions to remove obstacles or, better, cover all obstacles in your presentation.

- *Ask for the order.* The majority of salespeople fail to ask for the order. If you have covered all the prior suggestions, you will find it easy to close the sale. It's simple—just say, "Thank you, Mr. Jones. Do you want delivery today or tomorrow?"

The only real excuse for not buying is money. There is the story about the fellow who was asked to join in a game of poker. He said, "No, and I've got twelve reasons why I will not play with you." He was asked, "What are your reasons?" To which he replied, "Well, the first reason is that I don't have any money!" To which his card-playing friend replied, "Never mind the other eleven reasons." Top sales persuaders would find a way to get around this excuse for not "buying."

Fully aware that people are apt to be down on things they are not up on, well-trained and disciplined sales communicators know that they are *Professional Purchase Advisors for the customer and Business Builders for the company.*

Salespeople know that they are essentially an educator whose privileged mission is to banish ignorance and eliminate prejudices so people can enjoy the benefits of new and exciting innovations.

These then are the FUNdamentals of sales and communications. Come on in. You'll enjoy being your own boss, writing your own paycheck and making money. Okay. Now is the time to *Jump-Start Your Career and Your Life*—Yes You Can!

Index

QUANTITY	TITLE	PRICE	AMOUNT
_____	*How to Jump-Start Your Career,* **Robert L. Hemmings**	$19.95	_____
_____	*Follow That Customer,* **Egbert Jan van Bel/Ed Sander/Alan Weber**	$39.95	_____
_____	*Internet Marketing,* **Herschell Gordon Lewis**	$19.95	_____
_____	*Reliability Rules,* **Don Schultz/Reg Price**	$34.95	_____
_____	*The Marketing Performance Measurement Toolkit,* **David M. Raab**	$39.95	_____
_____	*Successful E-Mail Marketing Strategies,* **Arthur M. Hughes/Arthur Sweetser**	$49.95	_____
_____	*Managing Your Business Data,* **Theresa Kushner/Maria Villar**	$32.95	_____
_____	*Media Strategy and Planning Workbook,* **DL Dickinson**	$24.95	_____
_____	*Marketing Metrics in Action,* **Laura Patterson**	$24.95	_____
_____	*The IMC Handbook,* **J. Stephen Kelly/Susan K. Jones**	$49.95	_____
_____	*Print Matters,* **Randall Hines/Robert Lauterborn**	$27.95	_____
_____	*The Business of Database Marketing,* **Richard N. Tooker**	$49.95	_____
_____	*Customer Churn, Retention, and Profitability,* **Arthur Middleton Hughes**	$44.95	_____
_____	*Data-Driven Business Models,* **Alan Weber**	$49.95	_____
_____	*Creative Strategy in Direct & Interactive Marketing,* **Susan K. Jones**	$49.95	_____
_____	*Branding Iron,* **Charlie Hughes and William Jeanes**	$27.95	_____
_____	*Managing Sales Leads,* **James Obermayer**	$39.95	_____
_____	*Creating the Marketing Experience,* **Joe Marconi**	$49.95	_____
_____	*Coming to Concurrence,* **J. Walker Smith/Ann Clurman/Craig Wood**	$34.95	_____
_____	*Brand Babble: Sense and Nonsense about Branding,* **Don E. Schultz/Heidi F. Schultz**	$24.95	_____
_____	*The New Marketing Conversation,* **Donna Baier Stein/Alexandra MacAaron**	$34.95	_____
_____	*Trade Show and Event Marketing,* **Ruth Stevens**	$59.95	_____
_____	*Sales & Marketing 365,* **James Obermayer**	$17.95	_____
_____	*Accountable Marketing,* **Peter J. Rosenwald**	$59.95	_____
_____	*Contemporary Database Marketing,* **Martin Baier/Kurtis Ruf/G. Chakraborty**	$89.95	_____
_____	*Catalog Strategist's Toolkit,* **Katie Muldoon**	$59.95	_____
_____	*Marketing Convergence,* **Susan K. Jones/Ted Spiegel**	$34.95	_____
_____	*High-Performance Interactive Marketing,* **Christopher Ryan**	$39.95	_____
_____	*Public Relations: The Complete Guide,* **Joe Marconi**	$49.95	_____
_____	*The Marketer's Guide to Public Relations,* **Thomas L. Harris/Patricia T. Whalen**	$39.95	_____
_____	*The White Paper Marketing Handbook,* **Robert W. Bly**	$39.95	_____
_____	*Business-to-Business Marketing Research,* **Martin Block/Tamara Block**	$69.95	_____
_____	*Hot Appeals or Burnt Offerings,* **Herschell Gordon Lewis**	$24.95	_____
_____	*On the Art of Writing Copy,* **Herschell Gordon Lewis**	$34.95	_____
_____	*Open Me Now,* **Herschell Gordon Lewis**	$21.95	_____
_____	*Marketing Mayhem,* **Herschell Gordon Lewis**	$39.95	_____
_____	*Asinine Advertising,* **Herschell Gordon Lewis**	$22.95	_____
_____	*The Ultimate Guide To Purchasing Website, Video, Print & Other Creative Services,* **Bobbi Balderman**	$18.95	_____

Name/Title_____

Company _____

Street Address _____

City/State/Zip _____

Email _____ Phone _____

Credit Card: ☐ VISA ☐ MasterCard
☐ American Express ☐ Discover

☐ Check or money order enclosed (payable to Racom Communications in US dollars drawn on a US bank)

Subtotal	_____
Subtotal from other side	_____
8.65% Tax	_____
Shipping & Handling	_____
$7.00 for first book; $1.00 for each additional book.	
TOTAL	_____

Number _____ Exp. Date _____

Signature _____

Racom Communications, 150 N. Michigan Ave, Suite 2800, Chicago, IL 60601
312-494-0100, 800-247-6553, www. Racombooks.com